Almost Sincerely

Almost Sincerely

ZOË NORTON LODGE

First published in 2015
from the Writing & Society Research Centre
at the University of Western Sydney
by the Giramondo Publishing Company
PO Box 752
Artarmon NSW 1570 Australia
www.giramondopublishing.com

© Zoë Norton Lodge, 2015

Cover design and illustrations by
Georgia Norton Lodge
Page design by Harry Williamson
Typeset by Andrew Davies
in 11.25 / 14 pt Garamond 3

Printed and bound by Ligare Book Printers
Distributed in Australia by NewSouth Books

National Library of Australia
Cataloguing-in-Publication data:

Norton Lodge, Zoë
Almost Sincerely
ISBN 9781922146854 (pbk)

A823.4

For Yioryia, Wally-Pavlo, Andonia and The Gabro

Contents

1   Zoëtrope: Annandale

7   Nineteen-Eighty-Seven

15   A Metropolis of Fishes

27   Touching the Void

39   How Come Why For Did You
Call My Friend Denise a Bitch?

49   Madame Guillotine and
the Imitation Samoan

67   The Marron

75   Hats

83   The Birds

93   Phylly

105   Night of the Possums

117 An Open Letter of Apology
    to Little Georgia: Volume One

125 The Red Light

135 The Persistence of Memory

147 The Devil Wears a Denim
    Winter One-Piece

157 The Alive Pile

169 Day of the Dead

185 A Zoë's Christmas in Annandale

195 The Old Curiosity Shops

207 Petrol

217 Yia Yia on Papou

Zoëtrope: Annandale

Annandale: it's that skinny little suburb that fell asleep between good suburbs. Good suburbs where actual stuff happens like trips to the movies and catching the train.

If you were playing *SimCity* and you made Annandale, then you would need to get some bigger dreams and possibly some anti-depressants.

Let's take Annandale for a spin.

The long march of Johnston Street takes us from the Brothel and Guitar-Shop district of Parramatta Road all the way down to Rozelle Bay. Rozelle Bay where no ships come in. But before Johnston Street gets there it intersects the rumbling hubbub of Booth Street. And that's where the Annandale magic happens.

There you can buy tea bags and light bulbs and ham off the bone and peri-peri pizzas and cotton buds and beer and tulips and fancy fish and hot chips in newspaper. And nestled in amongst the practicalities are the diet supplement store and handicraft hell shops – the handicraft hell shops are all rubber kitchen utensils and sequined cardigans signifying nothing. And threaded quietly through all that are the Annandale zombies, the ancient milk bar with the new sign and the old burgers, the old burgers that sag into frowns in your hand and the TAB and the Vacuum Fixer and the Grocer with the Toupee.

Right *now*, if you're a malamute and you have two mums, and your two mums are architects, and they've tied you to the Trafalgar Street bus stop while they eat cultured butter on bread, bread too good for toasting, and drink coffee brewed for twelve hours served cold and revolting but nonetheless in a jar, then my friend, then you are an Annandale dog. If your lycra-pinched buttcrack bounces down Clover's new bike track as you whizz alongside Jubilee Park past a Pekaspaniel, a Jack-a-Poodle, a Labrakitty, then my friend, you're an Annandale dude.

But let's spin back, back just a little bit before in Annandale time…

If you're a forty year-old woman with bright red nails and all ten fingers be-ringed and jingle-jangle bangled wrists then you're Mamma screaming a fish-and-chips order to Dad who hasn't yet walked in the door from work, but he has thrown his jacket on a fence post and Mamma's stuffed his shirt pocket with a fist full of fivers and he's turned himself around to go and get the order and a half-bottle of Chardonnay. Little Georgia and I wave to him from the swing in the park across the street, and we swing to and fro until we get called inside which we know will be very soon for playtime is as sand through the egg-timer — about three minutes.

But in all our spinning we missed a few Annandale things. We missed the house where Sir Henry Parkes lived and the schoolrooms of St Mary Mackillop, we missed the charge of Old George Johnston and his Rum Rebellion. We missed the Annandale Street Sisters (suffragette and biological), Anne and Kath and Belle. We missed the Great Fire at the Canister Factory. We missed all of the schools and all of the churches and the teachers and children and pastors and sinners. We missed the Grand Old Abbey and the Witches' Houses, the aqueduct sewage system, the secession of the East Ward of Annandale, The Racophone and Kodak Factories and the Hunter Baillie Manse garden parties. We missed the Beale Piano Factory and in missing that, we missed that Annandale had pianos before it had electricity. Inside the factory we missed all the little fitters and joiners and turners, all the painters and pattern- and cabinet-makers, the veneer and brass and iron men, the timber yard and the mill, the rooms for drying and dusting and polishing and piano experiments. We missed the proudest most productive Piano Factory in the whole of the Empire and then we missed that it got turned into flats.

Here are some stories that might have happened to the people of Annandale, especially me. And some other stories that might have happened when me and my bumbag wished ourselves good luck and left the temperate climes of Annandale for a bit.

Nineteen-Eighty-Seven

So it's summer in 1987 and Annandale, a little suburb just tucked into the inner-western flap of mother Sydney, well Annandale see, it was changing.

From a snaggle-toothed, pock-marked, skid-marked man, passed out in a puddle of his own piss behind the wheel of a Mr Whippy van, to a beautiful gay man in his mid-twenties who works in a boutique advertising firm.

And me, well I was starting pre-school and goddamn it, I was going to be somebody.

I was going to rise out of the bog of Annandale like a lady in a swimming costume rises out of a cake, and I was gonna show 'em what I had. Cause I had something. That was for sure.

So it's summer in Annandale in 1987 and I got my shit packed, Mamma's making me a sandwich and cutting up a pear just how I like it. I'm ready to blow the house and skip out down to pre-school. Maybe pet a sweet dog on the way or some shit.

So Mamma and me we rock on down to Hilda Booler Pre-School. We're standing at the gates and I'm ready. I'm gonna mince in there and shake that building down. And then Mamma decides to come in the fucking gate.

'Mamma, seriously, I'm two and a half, you don't have to come in with me, that's really excessive,' I say. Because I could talk. I could talk real early, in a freakish fully-formed sentences kind of way. I'd be in my pram, wiggling or something, and people would put their fingers in my zone and I'd spit out my dummy and say:

'Hey lady, great loafers.'

So anyway, Mamma waits at the gates and I stroll on in and enrol myself in pre-school.

I have a sweet day. Eat some pears, make a picture with a potato cut in a star shape, make some new friends and shit my pants.

Now, when Mamma comes to pick me up at the end of the day she sees that I'm wearing different pants. Kirsty, the pretty teacher, who almost called DOCS when I enrolled myself in pre-school, has a quiet word to Mamma, and I realise I gotta think quick. I gotta think real quick or Mamma's gonna think I'm a fool. So as we leave and walk to the car I do something shifty.

'Mamma,' I say, 'Mamma, you're not going to believe this. But somebody *else* actually pooed in my pants.'

Mamma stares at me, and starts coughing real loud, like maybe she swallowed a fly or some shit. She's pretty amazed right, because it's pretty far out. So far out it had to be true.

'Really? Oh!' Mamma says.

Zoë one, Mamma zero.

Later that day she speaks for ages on the phone to Yia Yia and they're laughing a whole lot. I guess Papou must have done something real dumb like wiped his butt with a piece of toast. He always does dumb shit.

Anyway life on the beat was pretty charged. It was where I met Sally and Dwayne, who were real tough. Turned out they lived right across the street and pretty soon my parents and me were hanging out there a whole lot. At Sally and Dwayne's place there was a rifle down the side of the couch and one time after pre-school their dad gave us each a nip of Muscat. Sally's first word was 'arsehole'.

Sally and Dwayne were the ones who pulled the wool off my eyes about Uncle Kevin.

'How could Uncle Kevin be mine and Dwayne's uncle and also be your uncle?'

Sally and Dwayne and me were having a mad swing on the swings at pre-school.

'Yeah, I guess. I'd never thought about it like that.'

11

'They're lying to us,' said Dwayne. 'Uncle Kevin is their dealer.'

'Oh man!' I laughed. I'd been real naïve, I tried to change the subject quick sticks.

'So are your grandparents coming to pre-school today for Grandparents' Day?'

'Get real banana peel,' said Sally.

'No way man.'

'Hey isn't that your Yia Yia coming in the gates?' said Dwayne.

'No way man,' I said. Yia Yia started waving at me. Most grannies look pretty much the same, but there was no mistaking Yia Yia standing there with her big red hair and chunky silver heels, her green and purple elephant dress and her four million gold rings.

'Hey guys, I gotta take a slash, catch ya after nap time.' I ran to the toilets and stayed there for half an episode of *Playschool*.

When I came out Yia Yia was waiting for me. I made like she was demented and walked straight past her. Eventually Yia Yia had to use the phone and get Mamma to pick her up.

A few days later Mamma took me to Yia Yia's house. I knew I'd have some legwork to do.

Yia Yia and I were sitting at her countertop. She'd popped me a Just Juice and I knew she was about to ask why I'd been a little bitch at pre-school. So I got in first and hit the old lady in her soft spot.

'Yia Yia, can you teach me some Greek?'

'Of course Zoë!'

Too easy. Quick, think of something sensible.

'How do you say, "Can somebody please wipe my vagina?" in Greek?'

'Boriz-na Scoopi-ziz tu mooni moo, parakalo,' Yia Yia says. Then she starts coughing. That woman has to lay off those Alpine Lights.

She called Mamma and they laughed on the phone for ages. It was probably about Papou. Maybe about how he looks like someone tried to put King Gee stubbies on a Swiss ball, or how he rubs methylated spirits on his knees instead of going to the doctor. Yeah, I bet Papou did something real dumb last night like stuck his dick in the toaster. He always does dumb shit.

A bit later on Yia Yia had calmed down and we were setting up the kitchen to play Shops.

'Are you having fun at dance classes?' she asked me.

'Yia Yia, how else am I going to get on the stage?' I really wanted to get on the stage, get in on the action, sweat it out under the lights. I also wanted a job. I was getting tired of the rigmarole of pre-school. You come, you eat some Playdoh, you take a nap, you shit your pants. Day in, day out.

But life isn't a motherfucking dress rehearsal.

Mamma was working at Tourism Australia. And one day when she took me to work and asked me to draw

13

pictures of fairies or some bullshit I was like nah, fuck that, I'm gonna answer the phones. Apparently my phone skills were exemplary, and Mamma's boss thought I'd look really cute next to a koala. So that's how come I wound up as the pin-up toddler for Tourism Australia's Visit Down Under 1987 campaign in Japan. And I got paid shit-loads to eat a fucking ice-cream in front of the Harbour Bridge and pet a sweet wombat.

The ad game was pretty sweet for a while. You know you gotta hustle if you wanna make a dollar – and I was the best. I was the best at standing next to a kangaroo. I was the best at smiling next to Japanese people at the Opera House, I was the best at pointing at a kookaburra, I was the best at jumping next to a palm tree and I was the best at holding hands with a lifeguard. My team looked up to me and I helped them inspire themselves to inspire Japanese people to come over here and spend a metric fuck-ton of Yen.

But I was no diva, I had to get my education. And in a way I kind of missed the humdrum of cut-up pears and shit-smeared monkey bars.

So I told my team I had to split. They were like 'What will we do without you?' and I was like 'Don't worry, you'll find another porky white two-and-a-half year old whose eyes disappear when they smile.'

So I packed up my trailer and went back to pre-school to get my diploma and shit myself a few more times.

Fuck Nineteen-Eighty-Seven was a good year.

A Metropolis of Fishes

Until I was six years old I had no siblings and no pets. I had a TV in my room and I was allowed to eat as much cake as I wanted for afternoon tea, but neither the casually racist and pleasingly M15+ *Fast Forward*, that I watched unchecked, nor the oversized helpings of teacake drowning in clotted cream, adorned with a vanity strawberry, could clog the hole in my heart that ached for something smaller than me to take care of. I did have a life-sized doll called Molly. I used to take Molly to the park and tell everyone that she was my sister. If the fact that she was made from polyurethane didn't undo me, Molly's apparent African descent often betrayed my lie.

I was always looking for new more depressing forms of

self-delusion. After all, Molly's efforts at the seesaw were piss-weak and made me weight conscious. Sometimes my desperation for a companion would lead me down gloomy paths, like following little slivers of refracted light that would appear, briefly, as mini rainbows in the nooks between the windows and walls in my house. I would go up to my new friend, the light, and try to stroke it. I would get very close before my shadow would make it disappear, before I'd even had a chance to offer it a sip of my popper.

When Mamma invested in Tupperware she saw miles of leftovers from successful dinner parties stretching out before her. I saw the perfect home for a friendly slug. I took the smallest of the sealable containers to our little front garden and staked out our little front garden until I found one and put it in its plastic condo. Day after day, slug after slug would die in airtight domestic perfection. Then one day when a bag of mixed nuts required decanting, Slug House was repurposed forever.

Needless to say I was mentally ill-equipped at age six when the time for pets finally came.

Walking through level one of Grace Bros one wintery afternoon, I stepped a little heavier, and breathed a little like I had a breathing problem as I allowed myself to imagine the explosion of positive consequences that were about to befall me, when I would go into the pet shop and get me a fish.

The announcement that now, after years of solitude, I

could get a fish, came at dinner the night before. We were in the dining room, on one of the rare occasions that dinner had moved away from the lounge room and into this other place, where Nicky Buckley and Tony Barber were a mere muted glow from the telly in the kitchen. Mamma and Dad sat together opposite me. Dad was wearing his familiar outfit of suit pants and belt, slippers, singlet and waistcoat. His face was an anxious furrow which was slowly courting a more relaxed sheen of Chardonnay-sweat. Mamma was fierce in her I-work-at-home-but-I'm-ready-for-anything-wear which included giant cork heels with gold straps that criss-crossed all the way up her calves, a fitted hounds-tooth skirt and bright orange blouse to match her amber earrings and necklace set. All tied together with a big gold belt.

They sat opposite me, observing with a measure of concern as I ate at double speed, decorating my part of the table with mincemeat and soggy risoni, enthusiastic, was I, to the point of mild fetishism about pasta.

'Zoë,' said Dad, 'Zoë, stop eating for a minute.'

I stopped chewing, leaving a chipmunk's stash of pasta gunk and meat in each of my cheeks.

'Yeah?' I ventured through the mush.

'We've decided that you can get a fish.'

My eyes widened to match my cheeks and I gasped, expelling dinner everywhere. So this was happiness.

As we walked into the shop, the very next day, I let go of Mamma's hand. I was blind to the grotty rubber floors,

19

to the aromatics of rot and gunge and the juvenile green texta markings on each tank, smudgily articulating the cost of each type of fish. All I could see were neon greens and oranges and highlighter pinks and yellows, electric blues, fire-alarm reds, Grimace-from-McDonald's purples and every other colour in my Derwent-pencil dreams, all rushing through the tanks that lined the walls, stacked one atop the other: a metropolis of fishes. They had places to be those fishes, overtaking the street-sweeper snails who slowly made their way across the glass, apparently cleaning it with their rejuvenating slime.

'What kind a tank you got?' said the fifteen-year-old fish fuckwit.

'Actually this is our first fish,' said Mamma, which embarrassed me tremendously. This person need not know that we were so ill-versed in the Book of Fish.

'Ok, so do you want a tropical tank or a fresh-water tank? Fresh water is good for first-timers and kids,' he said looking at me. I knew what it felt like to be patronised. It felt like a little stream of hot, fresh wee trickling down my face.

'Ok that sounds great,' said Mamma, and she started walking with the man to the other side of the shop, past all the swirling, tropical utopia of my dreams to where the fresh-water fish were. The sad, partially sedated, floating towards the top of the tank in amongst acres of pink stringy shit fresh-water fish.

'This one looks a bit like you,' I said under my breath, to Mamma, pointing to one of the googly-eyed greying fish. Mamma had a thyroid problem.

'Let's take that one,' I said, pointing at Mamma in fish form.

It is very easy to adjust to improvement. No sooner had I walked into pre-school for the first time, than that delicious aching to go there melted away and in its place a sense of entitlement festered. Later, when I would acquire a sister after six years of lonely yearning, mere weeks after her birth when physics forbade her fitting fashionably into Molly's clothes, I would decree her to be essentially pointless. And having wished so hard for a pet, wished so hard that at some point I had actually sought affection in some bit of light briefly coursing across a wall, I was crestfallen when, having been exposed to the tropical cornucopia, all I could have was a floppy and melancholic boring-coloured shit-fish whose only recommendation was that she looked a bit like Mamma.

The fish fuckwit put Mamma 2.0 in a plastic bag, and fastened it with sticky-tape. I picked out a pile of rainbow stones and a little plastic tank and we took her home.

I kept the fish on my desk next to my homework. I named it Googley, but its secret name was Mamma. Almost immediately, its tank took on a greying mouldy quality and a light stench began to fill my room. I sort of liked feeding it the little orange flakes, which tasted, I learned privately, like salty leaves. And even though I hated it for everything it wasn't, Googley became the proud first stop on a tour of my bedroom, which went roughly: fish, bed, jar of sweets on mantlepiece, rest of mantle-piece, chair, box of disorderly Polly Pockets, desk, notice-board, door. I got to give that tour exactly once to my friend Sally, before the fish died a week after purchase. I woke up in the morning and there was Mamma, floating upside down at the top of the little tank, her giant brassy eyes, staring forever at nothing in particular.

No great sadness overcame me. However, my parents started behaving like I was made of fairy floss, liable to crumple into a tiny wet ball at the slightest criticism. This had a causal relationship with the fact that I was no longer being asked to brush my teeth or have a bath or undertake any of the other personal hygiene chores pinned to the noticeboard above my desk. The next evening we went to Grace Bros again, this time as a trio, Mamma, Dad and I, arm in arm, credit card in pocket. Now we weren't first-timers. We were guilt-riddled second-timers, ready to upscale.

My parents had learned some valuable lessons from round one. Fish die unexpectedly and often, therefore, a populate-or-perish approach is best practice. To that end, always have at least seven fish, so that their attrition can go largely unnoticed. The best home for the fish is in the palliative care of the dining room, where any morning carcasses can be swiftly removed without anybody noticing, except Dad the undertaker.

That afternoon we came home with a big fish tank made of glass, loads of garish stones, various ornaments, several uncategorised sea-plants, and two bags of fish ranging from beige to bland in colour. We also got some of those cleaning snails and an electric filter. At home I arranged the neon stones in the tank and placed all the little toys in there purposefully. A mini statue of a ghost, a never-spinning red windmill and a little sparkly blue robot were all imbedded in the stony turf, amongst the slimy, waving plants. We filled her up and let the little fish float in their bags at the top of the tank. When we felt as though they had become well-adjusted, we released them into the taste-less, glittering captivity of the rest of their lives.

The next death happened the morning after.

A fat pinkish fish had gotten stuck behind the electric filter and all its bits had smooshed together, fatally so. Despite the significant effort that had gone into preventing this set of circumstances, I was the first to chance upon its perverse misshapen corpse. I showed Dad, who gently prised it out from behind the filter with his bare hands, put it in a teacup, and then commenced digging with one finger what would soon become a tiny mass grave in our garden.

'That one was called Mildred,' I told Dad as we buried it in the little patch of designated dirt. It didn't have a name, but I thought calling it after Dad's sick mother had a certain loftiness that he would appreciate.

The limitations of the fish quickly became irritating. Aside from eating, wiggling, shitting and dying, those little slimy blobs were capable of nothing. One day when I had some friends round after school, I made the fraught claim that I had trained my fish to follow some basic commands.

'Go on then,' said Dwayne standing next to the tank of sadness, eating a Cadbury Furry Friend. Her eyes glowered at me.

Without a plan, I put an index finger on the side of the tank, in the vicinity of a motley carp, and followed it round its aimless journey hoping it would look like it was following me. Which it wasn't.

'Get real,' said Sally.

'They did it better before.' I mumbled. 'Anyway, they're pretty stupid, let's go to the park.'

My cheerless attempts to bond with my fish had become too awful even for me. After that, any mixed or mild emotions I had towards them crystalised into hatred.

And yet, still, the fish came and died and rotted in the garden in a meaningless and expensive cycle. Nobody wanted them. They stank which upset Mamma, and Dad would spend the better part of every Saturday siphoning the water out of the tank, which was revolting, and somehow couldn't be done without using his mouth. To me, they had come to represent inertia and disappointment. Yet somehow we were fish people now, and we would diligently replace the dead, week in, week out, without question, for a great many years.

During the heady summer between Years Six and Seven a cat wandered into our house and set up shop. We were mid-renovation, pushing the limits of our house as far into our tiny courtyard as Council would permit. Wherever that cat had been before, it considered hanging out in an active construction site an improvement. We took it to the vet, who told us that she would shove it in the window for a fortnight and if nobody came to take pity on her in that time she'd get the needle. I had already named it – Magic Scratch Patch Heart. That, and the impending execution, had a weakening effect on my parents' courage and we were allowed to keep it. Magic Scratch Patch Heart was not unlike a traumatised foster-child. Displaced, terrified and finding my overblown attempts to behave like her mother unsettling and altogether too soon. She also gave me ringworm.

Georgia didn't understand my maladapted love for Magic Scratch Patch Heart. She had been born into a world altogether different from mine. She already had a sister for one, and more importantly those hateful fish were already there. For her, more so than the rest of us, the fish were just happenstance, like the recycling bin. And just like the recycling bin, she never thought to ask if they had a purpose.

Some time after the arrival of the PTSD-suffering cat, laziness won the day, and we stopped replacing the fish in the tank. When the last one died Dad took the fish tank to the tip. We watched him raise the thing high above his head and then hurl it into the landfill.

And Dad's mouth slowly recovered from the siphoning-induced ulcers, and the house finally stopped smelling like the sea had died.

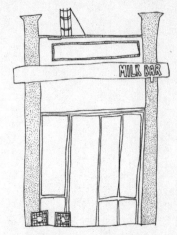

Touching the Void

Across the road from our house in Annandale there is a little corner shop. The shop sells one kind of ice-cream and tampons and the newspaper on special occasions. There is a big vinyl sign plastered across the shopfront which depicts the disembodied head of a smiling old lady. Where her body might have been it says 'We Sell Grandma Maude's Famous Pies'. But nobody has heard of Grandma Maude, and if there is a lovely pie warmer steaming with baked treats somewhere inside, I've certainly never clocked it. It's seen off several great leaders, that little corner shop. Tassos, famous for hitting his wife and saying 'All rice has maggots in it, you just have to pick them out', is long gone, and his sad commercial empire that he passed onto Ahmed and Mina and their seven children, was passed on again to a man my parents called Soft Hands. And with this change, the ancient dusty tins of dolmades in brine and children out of breath from playing hand clappies and making friendship bracelets out of fresh fettuccini on the bitumen floor were replaced by a ruthless economy and distrust of the human condition.

Why stock all the kinds of bread when you could stock one loaf of mystery bread? Vegemite is black viscous sin and cans of tuna are cat food anyway and cat food is cheaper and toilet paper is French and milk is extravagant and probably sexual and customers who want milk can go up the street to the Grocer with the Toupee and pick up a litre and drink it right out of the bottle with a prostitute and piss their futures into the wind, thinks Soft Hands to himself, in his darned black trousers and crisp, white business shirt, as he clasps a broom with his soft fingers and sweeps the dry, bare concrete out the front of his shop and he wonders why the children don't come by any more for the one type of sweet he sells as he sweeps at nothing in particular as he looks across the road to our house and glowers because he is discomfited by Mamma who yelled at him for putting rubbish in our bin with his tickly soft hands.

But Mamma doesn't have time for his shit right now. It's a balmy Friday springtime afternoon. The jasmine and lavender have coloured Annandale in bustling purple and pinkish-white and Mamma has somewhere to be. She has to go across the park, which is swirling this afternoon with all of the young mums and their very little ones, and down to the school to pick me up from Year Two camp.

Mamma gets to the school and she waits at the big old iron gates. At first she waits because she's thirty minutes early, as is her custom. But then as the other mothers and fathers arrive she waits and waits. And she waits until even after the more booze-addled adults have remembered to arrive for their sprogs. And they all wait with patience. And then less so.

And then the principal comes out in her bright orange two-piece suit. She is kindly, and stout and smiling through a panic attack, because in all of her decades as principal, nothing like this has ever happened before. And out she comes to address the emerging parental frustration and says that she's really very sorry but there has been an incident on one of the buses on the way home. That's all she knows. Mamma is first responder. 'What kind of incident?' But the principal says she doesn't know. Now Mamma is standing nose-to-nose with the principal and she is screaming 'Well which bloody kids were on the bus?' and the principal doesn't know this either and she excuses herself to 'find out more' returning to her informationless office to drink gin from her teapot and worry a fair bit and weather the storm of parents raging outside.

And me? Well I'd been glad to get out of that humdrum doldrum. I was sick of the frowning burgers of Annandale and glad to get down the highways and byways as far-aways as I could get from Annandale, a great forty-eight kilometres to be exact to the fabricated bushland tracks and the wooden-esque cabins of school camp. Sure the general social torment of Year Two was more concentrated on school camp, but I was ready to embrace *les différences*. I was ready to have an anxiety attack in the open air while pretending to use a compass, sailing a paper boat in the lake and not riding the horses.

Things were so different on school camp. I ate cold spaghetti jaffles and drank warm apple-juice poppers for breakfast at the very long tables, lined with all my comrades, all of us glad to be out of our uniforms and into colourful Mambo shorts and tie-dyed T-shirts. I did things I thought a girl-guide would do, like making the most of my sleeping bag which on the down side had a stabby zipper but as a plus, had a sealed base which made a perfect hidey hole for the cellophane-wrapped sticky, melting contraband I would sneak-eat at night while my bunk buddies Janie and Alex and Madeleine were sleeping. I cried when my swimsuit strap broke, I cried when I sucked at orienteering, I cried during three out of five trips to the toilet and while I ate my chewy candy of solitude in my sleeping bag. I made a skirt out of streamers and won the talent quest with Janie for our a cappella rendition of *Accidentally Kelly Street* for which we were each awarded toffee apples whose impenetrable sticky, green crust saved us from their rotting insides.

It's the end of school camp and I'm holding hands with Janie ready to get on our allocated Year Two bus. And then up comes Mr McGregor in his chinos and short-sleeved shirt and tie. 'This bus is full,' says Mr McGregor, plainly. Then, with no apparent regard for the pre-made whosie-sitsie-next-to-who-on-the-bus arrangements, he sends some of us off to the Year Four bus. Just as we're getting on, Janie looks at me and through the chunk of her blonde hair which she is twirling in her mouth, Janie says, 'Look. The driver is an Oldy Mouldy Shit Man.'

We walk down the aisle but there are no two seats next to each other. As Janie disappears to the other end of the bus she mouths, *We're going to have a crash.*

I'm sitting down at the back of the stupid Year Four bus next to stupid Bronwyn from Year Four whose face is plastered with pink zinc in an effort to cling onto the memories of camp, and far away from my friend Janie, and I'm staring at Mr Smythe bending over the seat in front of me. Nice Mr P&C Smythe whose wife runs the school canteen. He's gotten on because he's just remembered he had his son Benji's puffer in his pocket. He's not supposed to be on this bus, he explains to Benji, but he's just remembered about the puffer. And I'm glazed-over half-tuned into this boring audio when Mr Smythe stands bolt upright. His squat little middle-aged man-form stands as bolt upright as can be. He stands bolt upright because something isn't right.

Mr Smythe screams 'FUCK,' he screams 'FUCK, FUCK, FUCK, FUCK,' as he runs in his orienteering shorts all the way down to the front of the bus. As he's running down the bus we look out the window and notice a telegraph pole gliding incrementally away to our left. And we don't think too much of it, we just know that Mr Smythe started yelling 'FUCK' and never stopped yelling it which makes us laugh.

From outside the bus the teachers watch on and the bus driver watches on. Oldy Mouldy Shit Man who didn't put the handbrake on when he got off the bus to check the tyres holds his **OMSM** hands to his **OMSM** face. The adults all look on helpless and pointing as the bus picks up speed. And then it begins to descend the slope and career towards the lake.

The bus is getting faster and the lake is getting closer and Mr Smythe must be thinking *I need to stop the bus* and he sees what might be an empty bus in his periphery. I cross my faltering heart that it's empty and not full of kids because it's way too late for the brakes but we don't know what he's thinking, we don't know what's happening as Mr Smythe spins the wheel and crashes our bus into the other bus. And he realises that blessed stupid bus was empty and that he just saved fifty kids from drowning and we see him lean his body on the steering wheel as he exhales and he laughs.

I'm still laughing as I gently plop onto my multi-purpose sleeping bag on the aisle of the bus and everyone is laughing about Mr Smythe yelling 'FUCK'. Everyone is cheering because swearing is the best. Because watching fat little Mr Smythe run down the bus screaming 'FUCK' was the best.

We think it's the funniest ever until someone says 'bus crash'. Until someone says, 'We've been in a *bus crash*. Hey guys, we've been in a *bus crash*.' Then we realise we've been in a *bus crash*.

Suddenly everyone is crying. 'Ow!' Stupid Bronwyn from Year Four sitting next to me starts screaming. 'I hurt my thumb in the *bus crash*.'

I am realising I didn't plop gently out of my seat onto a sleeping bag when Mr Smythe was yelling 'FUCK'. No. I was *thrown*. I was *thrown* out of my seat. And hardly onto a sleeping bag. Onto the *floor*. Perhaps fatally so. I had touched the void.

I take a moment's break from considering my broken body and see Janie. She's looking back at me, still sucking on her hair. *I told you so* she mouths before screaming 'I fainted!'

A vanity ambulance comes to survey the scene. The children who now know they've been in a *bus crash* are sprawled out and crying all over the green. A great many more children than had been on the bus are now prone on the ground clutching bits of their bodies. Anna Jackson, captain of the senior netball team, gets to go in the ambulance because she's convinced the ambulance man she has a concussion. She's good, Anna Jackson, she's real damn good.

It's after dark before we get back to Annandale, boring old Annandale where nobody crashes buses. And all the Mothers and Dads are waiting at the gates.

I step off the bus with the solemnity of someone who has been *thrown* out of their seat and onto the *floor* in a *bus crash*.

'Zoë!' Mamma gives me a big squeeze.

'Mamma. I was *thrown* onto the *floor* of the bus in the *bus crash*!'

'Oh my god!' she screams, and holds me close.

Later that evening we go down the street, to the bit of Annandale where the shops are, and everyone we pass, Mrs Jones watering her bizzy lizzies, Suzie with a stick picking dog shit off her shoe, Arthur closing up the Hoover Fixer and the Grocer with the Toupee, and to everyone we see Mamma says 'Zoë was *thrown* onto the *floor* of the bus in the *bus crash*,' and when she tells Johnno at the milk bar he gives me a million hot chips with my sad drooping burger.

When I get home, Dad is there. He's just gotten changed out of his work suit into his favourite singlet and flower-covered drawstring pants which Mamma has banned him from leaving the house in. He doesn't know anything of the *bus crash* or the *throwing* or the *floor*. Because he's been at work all day he doesn't even know.

'There was a *bus crash* and Zoë was *thrown* onto the *floor* in the *bus crash*!' says Mamma, seriously.

'I was *thrown* onto the *floor*!' I say.

Dad asks us to slow down, he can't understand us, but his eyes are wide.

'There was a *bus crash*?'

'Yes,' I say. 'A *Bus. Crash.*'

'Is everyone alright?'

'I was *thrown.*'

'But you're okay?'

'Onto the *floor*!'

I start jumping up and down mortified at his calming-downess.

'No! I am not okay!'

'Where does it hurt?'

I pause. I'm so mad, I can't even think.

'Everywhere. *EVERY. WHERE.*' I say plunging my angry little hand into the soggy bag of chips.

'Well at least you have an appetite.'

'Hardly.' I say stuffing another handful of sloppy chips in my mouth.

'I probably won't even be able to finish these.'

'Well give them to me then,' says Dad and he snatches the chips out of my hand. I look at Mamma, horrified. She looks at Dad and she is so mad at him she doesn't even need to say any words. And he looks at me and gives them back.

'You'll be fine,' he says.

'Dad?'

'Yeah?'

'You're a big poo.'

And Mamma makes an exception to the flower pants rule and sends Dad across the street to Soft Hands' shop, looking like a man whom nobody loves, to buy me a recuperating Magnum.

'I heard there was a *bus crash*?' says Soft Hands to Dad, who hates him, as he hands the Magnum over the counter.

'It's fine.'

'Is your daugther okay?' says Soft Hands, lightly tickling the Magnum packet with his supple wriggling fingers.

'She'll be fine.'

'Another Dad came in and said his little girl was hurt so I gave them a free ice-cream.'

This was an unprecedented gesture of empathy and neighbourliness from Soft Hands to which Dad was unaccustomed. Still, he knows an opportunity.

'Ah well, Zoë was *thrown* onto the *floor* of the bus in the *bus crash*,' said Dad, slowly putting his wallet back in his pocket. 'Also I had a shit day at work, will you spot me a packet of Pall Mall Milds?'

'Greed is a sin,' says Soft Hands with a wan smile, adjusting the curiously ostentatious cufflinks on his pristine white shirt. And then he emits a sharp, singular sound, which Dad thinks might have been a laugh. Like the laugh of someone who had no idea what a laugh sounded like but that nonetheless had a ring of sincerity to it. And Dad does a little laugh back. And he leaves with his charity Magnum and a new appreciation for Soft Hands.

How Come Why For Did You Call
My Friend Denise a Bitch?

Mamma was one strict lady when I was growing up. Playtime at the park directly next to our house was limited to short spurts in high daylight and supervised by Mamma, who could see me always through all the windows along the east wing of our family home. It didn't matter whether she was knitting a scarf, making a Nescafé or watching *Wheel of Fortune*. Whatever she was doing, she was also watching me in the park. Trees were not for climbing and legs were not for running. That's how I grew up to be in a rare subset of ethnically Mediterranean people with the pallor of jellyfish. Should a sleepover be on the cards, Mamma always required a detailed itinerary of any goings on and their proximity to major roads and rapists and I was walked to school until long after I developed the ability to menstruate.

If horror films have taught us anything, it's those sleepy little suburbs where nothing much ever happens, where the doors are always unlocked and the children unwatched, it's those types of places, the world's Annandales, where the terrible thing will definitely happen. Now, Mamma didn't really like horror movies. She was more of a *Judge Judy* type of woman. But lessons are everywhere, and *Judge Judy* taught a very similar syllabus on the perils of living in a boring residential postcode.

And then one day, after twelve steely years of watching and waiting, the moment came that Mamma had been preparing for all my life.

I was playing in the park with my long-term collaborators Sally and Dwayne. We'd been tight since pre-school and the main base for our operations was the park between our houses. There were further (temporary) members of our council, but if we three were there then quorum was met and we could discuss business – which usually focussed on matters such as which of the dogs that always fought in the park would die first, whose parents were *real* alcoholics and which were fair-weather benders, who currently had cake in their house and which teachers were probably having sex with each other and which others should be fired for being perverts.

One autumn, Year-Six day, we were sitting up the top

of the slippery dip discussing whose dad was the most drunkest the most often. It was definitely a close race, we all agreed, but nonetheless each passionately advocated our personal dad to be the most loaded the most regularly. I was quietly prosecuting the case for my own dad – pointing to the sneakiness of his drinking many half-bottles of Chardonnay as evidence in favour of his superiority over Sally and Dwayne's dad when I heard someone calling from the bottom of the slide.

'Oi!'

It was an older girl. She had straight red hair that had been pulled over and over through an iron, possibly a clothes iron because it was baked and cauterised at the tips. From the very middle of her forehead, two tiny plaits sprung out of her hairline and arced down her face, weighted at the bottom with pink baubles. She had brutal pencil lines where her eyebrows might have been and she had undone all the bottom buttons of her white school blouse and tied it in a knot, exposing an infected yin-yang belly-button ring.

She was standing just in front of another girl, whose school kilt was high and tight and framed by a jumper that was tied around her waist. She wore a pink plastic crucifix that nestled into her significant cleavage and her dyed black hair was tied so tightly into a bun as to give her the impression of having had too much work done. Everything about them was remote and discomforting. Whatever these

43

things were, they weren't from Annandale.

'I said oi! Girl!'

'What?' I said.

She looked up at me at the top of the slippery dip.

'Tell me how come why for did you call my friend Denise a bitch?'

'Who's *Denise?*' I said, with an inflection that implied that I did not think Denise was a nice name, even though I secretly did, and also had the effect of seeming like I hadn't even noticed her friend, even though I definitely had.

'Get down here,' she said.

And me, with the confidence of someone who has always lived in Annandale, who knows that nothing bad ever happens in the park slid down and stood in front of the teenage miscreants, arms folded.

'I didn't even say *anything*,' I said.

The girl's eyes widened. The other girl, who I presumed was Denise, didn't look at me. She just picked the day's filth out of her long, pink nails.

'How come why for are you now calling my friend Denise a liar?'

'*What?*' I said, and the girl raised her arm. She raised her arm, dripping with glowing, glittery plastic bracelets, she pulled it back and then, before I had any idea what was happening slapped me hard across the face, digging her acrylic nails into my cheek and dragging them across in her follow through.

I looked at her. Completely stunned. I never knew that there could be any negative consequences for just telling the truth. But there I was. All slapped.

I was about to stammer out something. I had no idea what it was going to be, when the other girl, Maybe-Denise, ran at me gridiron style, her massive boobs swinging wildly, like angry pendulums as she closed in and pushed me backwards into the dirt.

And that was the moment.

All the autumn leaves on the ground began to rustle and all the little blades of grass in the park stiffened beneath them. The clouds in the sky thickened as they drew closer together then joined and everything became dull.

Then a huge gust of wind blew through the park. It blew all the way through the park to my house and it blew the front door of my house wide open.

And there was Mamma standing in the doorway of our house and she was bright. Everything else was grey, but Mamma was bright. She was bright because she was backlit by every scented candle in Annandale, flaming behind her down the hallway of our house. And she stood still, as the wind swirled the little lit wicks of the candles behind her and the trees around the house and all the autumn leaves on the ground in the park and the last of the leaves that were still in the trees all swirled in the wind, but Mamma stood still, her eyes locked on us, on the mess in the park that we were.

And as we watched her, she slowly parted her arms, dripping in the black silk of her *Judge-Judy*-watching kimono and she splayed out all of her ten ringed fingers. She looked those two girls dead in the eyes as she bent her knees and sprung off the front porch and into the air.

Mamma was in the air, and she was flying. She flew over our gate and across the road and into the park, darting through the trees, twisting and turning, her black kimono flying out behind her, her black hair flying out behind her and her espadrilles never even almost touching the pavement.

And she flew way above us. Way above me on the ground and above Maybe-Denise and the other one and even above Sally and Dwayne at the top of the slippery slide.

And she hovered above us, spinning, around us all, in a slow circle. She spun above her prey, above her treasured ward and above the spectators. She could have grabbed them there and then, her prey, but that was no fun, Mamma wanted to see some bitches run.

Maybe-Denise got up and started to run. And then the other one did too. They started to run through the park and just as they were about to disappear out of sight, Mamma began to fly, faster than before, her arms and legs stretched out as she glided through the air breaking every speed limit of every transport that ever was. She was bat and she was bullet streaming through the air and then out of the park and down the hill and out of our sight.

Sally and Dwayne and I looked at each other.

'Your mum is really mad,' said Dwayne.

'Yeah,' I said, solemnly.

'And I'll tell you something, I'll never be able to play in the park again.'

'Ever,' added Sally.

A few minutes later we saw the two girls walking back into the park, trying desperately not to look frightened. Mamma was behind them, marching them forward, a hand pressed into each of their backs, and then she sat them both down on a park bench.

'You girls are in deep shit,' she said, leaning against a tree.

'Sally go to your house and call the cops.'

'What?' said Maybe-Denise.

'Don't even call the cops!' said the other one.

'You, don't talk,' said Mamma. 'You okay?' she asked me.

'Yeah, I'm fine.'

'Don't wash your face, don't wash anything until the cops come and take a photo of your injuries.'

'She wasn't *injured*,' said Maybe-Denise.

'I. Said. Don't. Talk. I've missed the second case of *Judge Judy* now, and I'm not in the mood to hear your voice,' said Mamma, still leaning against the tree and not looking at Maybe-Denise.

The police came and took the girls away. They were pleading and crying and Mamma watched on, glistening with hero-sweat and smoking a Pall Mall Mild, with a distinct absence of mercy in her eyes.

After that I really thought I would never be able to play in the park again. That wasn't entirely true, but Mamma made Dad go have his after-work half-bottles of Chardonnay in the park with Sally and Dwayne's dad every day after that.

This was pretty good, because our Dads were not as good at knowing what we were and weren't supposed to be doing. Also it made it much easier for us to decide who was the most drunkest every day.

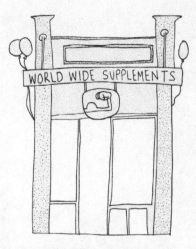

Madame Guillotine and
the Imitation Samoan

When Sir Henry Parkes, Alfred Deakin, Edmund Barton and their less memorable mates sat down at the Fathers of Federation moot-cum-sausage-sizzle, it was decreed that in our great country no two families that were in any way compatible should live within cooee of one another. 'Neighbours must,' espoused Deakin, through a mouthful of coleslaw and Wonder White, 'Neighbours must always be fucking weirdos.'

Sir Henry Parkes, who was actually a resident of Annandale, knew this to be a steadfast truism, and the rule has remained rigorously adhered to, at least in that little village, from time immemorial. True story: Parkes lived in Annandale in a house called Kenilworth that looked like a witch's hat. Mark Twain stayed there when Mark Twain made his presumably disappointing visit to Annandale. And so it goes, that our family, if little else, were definitely a bunch of neighbours.

My parents loved playing games like Pictionary and Bridge with local folk. They loved eating take-away Thai in the park opposite our house with whoever was there. They loved forcing Georgia and me to become friends with some alcoholic's offspring. They loved barbeques, dinner parties, movie nights, afternoon teas. They also loved giving our neighbours highly offensive nicknames and operating in ways intended to make them move house.

It was a safe assumption that somewhere, amongst the hodgepodge of new couples trickling into the street, at any given time, there was at least one house marked with an invisible X. Eventually, following some murky circumstances, they'd move out and soon enough another couple would arrive, in strange suburban Noah's ark-dom, and this would continue in perpetuity. When we started learning about fractions in school, I began to wonder whether it was possible that my parents were some sort of denominator.

Then one night in Year Ten, as I lay in bed mesmerised by the comic-book good looks and soothing tones of Jeff Probst pulsing tenderly out of my television, everything clicked into place. I was actually trapped in season after season of *Survivor: Annandale*.

Which looked something like this.

Episode One: A removalist truck ambles through the mighty lavender-lined streets and dog-shit littered avenues of Annandale until it settles somewhere within sight of our place, AKA basecamp, thus heralding the beginning of the season. So long as the destination is a house on our street, or visible from ours, or in part connected through a shared back fence, or close enough that a renovation could occur and we would be aware through visual or aural cues, then the locale is sufficiently proximal for *Survivor: Annandale* to commence. Basecamp's sentry (Mamma) watches intently as cargo is unloaded, chair after cupboard, from the truck into the temporary holdings of these transient players. Sentry brings back a comprehensive report from the move, detailing items such as: one x birch-wood (veneer only) coffee table, stained; one x curtain in mismatched colour to one x couch.

Episode Two: My parents now know exactly how much Carlton Ware is in the temporary holdings, but they do not yet know the names of the campers. So, like little woodworms into the oak-esque bookcase, my parents will now deeply ingratiate themselves into the lives of the unsuspecting newcomers. My parents will help clean their gutters, feed their kids home-made grape icy-poles, be not un-nice to their dog when it treads shit through our house, drink with them on weeknights and share stories from the old country (Dad: Wales; Mum: Carlingford) and start a regular custom of playing a board or card game –

depending on their skillset, intelligence, propensity to getting wasted, propensity to losing their cool.

Episode Three: After settling into this routine for anything ranging from weeks to years, they begin to scrutinise the temporary residents for deep character and behavioural flaws, possibly over Scrabble game-play, home extension plans threatening to block our 'view of the city', parenting techniques, dubious past, too-contrived Christmas wreath on front door, misspeaking or not bringing wine.

Episode Four: The die has been cast, and it's time to enter a new phase where the relationship between my parents and the passers-through sours sours like a paddle-pop abandoned on a slippery dip at high noon. The onset is signified when my parents bestow upon these now incurably awful people a nickname. Notable past examples include Janice Underbids, for a bad Bridge player; Maggot, for a man who persisted with a renovation even though my parents had successfully blocked it with Council; Pony, for a woman who my parents genuinely mistook for a pony walking down Trafalgar Street because, allegedly, her giant round buttocks trapped in brown corduroy trousers, as she bent over to adjust her velcro walking shoes, gave the distinct impression from half a block back that she was, in fact, a pony; Paedophile, the man who spent too long watching me and my friends try to do acrobatics in the park; Soft Hands, the man who worked in the shop opposite, a shop that didn't really sell anything as a rule and was tended by a man with particularly soft-milky hands; Yoghurt and Baked Potato, a fat couple who would have called themselves that during intercourse, apparently.

Episode Five: After the nickname has steeped into common parlance, and the birth names are all but forgotten, watch as the relationship slowly deteriorates, and just when it seems to have bottomed out completely, enter a phase of volatility, where behaviour is unpredictable and interactions are at best intolerably awkward. Now is the time, for example, to instigate a loud row with the nomads usually in the park or in line for fish and chips, or in the middle of the road.

Episode Six: In an ideal world, this episode takes place at the itinerants' auction which my parents will consider attending for the dual rewards of intimidating them, and telling potential buyers that the property is riddled with termites. This occasionally leads to the desired outcome: neighbours sell the house for less than market value.

Episode Seven: Vagabonds move to *Sto Thiavolou Tou Goulou Manna* – which translates roughly from very broken Greek as 'The Devil's Arsehole', but means to Mamma any suburb that isn't Annandale. And my parents win. *Fin*.

My parents rocked at this game. Because they invented it. And they were the only ones who knew they were playing, a distinct advantage. In fact there was only one season of *Survivor: Annandale* that was really a contest. My Parents vs Madame Guillotine and The Imitation Samoan.

Named so because she was French and a bitch, and he, despite his claims, didn't really appear to be Samoan, or at least not *very* Samoan. There is no denying that these were amongst the most unnecessarily racist appellations gifted to any of our neighbours, but the pair was part of an elite category of players who were objectively knob-heads. This round was closely fought, and the final outcome wasn't entirely clear – it may be different depending on whose history books you read. My parents always won *Survivor: Annandale*, because they understood a thing about endurance. But Madame Guillotine knew about war.

They moved in one high-school spring. Just ten houses down. Cast-iron garden furniture, red child's bed shaped like a motor-car, bounty of videos, trampoline and ten boxes labelled 'wine'. From the initial sentry's report, these seemed like the kind of people we would like to know. On the day they moved in, our army ventured out to survey. Pizza menu in hand.

When we got to the front gate, loud rockabilly tunes beat out of a stereo and a small, sweaty, pink-skinned man with two chins supporting a stubbly smile came to greet us, swathed in a sweaty wife-beater, fag in mouth.

'We live up the street,' said Mamma.

'Yeah, I saw you before come past with your notebook,' he said.

'We thought you might like some pizza?' ventured Dad, holding up the ancient paper menu.

'Oh shit yeah. Come the hell in, yeah?' he said, bidding us to follow him inside.

'I'm Mick. This is me wife Carla and little Tom is running around upstairs somewhere.'

Carla had miles of red hair, cascading down into brittle coarse ends right at her bum.

'Girls, you go now and meet little Tom Tom upstairs,' she said, with a thick French accent.

Georgia and I made our way up the paisley-carpeted staircase, musty in the dusty wake of moving boxes. At the top we found ourselves in Tom's room. He was sitting on his red car-bed throwing Iced Vovos at the wall. Tom was nice, for a three year old, and he didn't even smell the fear hormones I usually emitted talking to toddlers. Or if he did, he politely ignored them like a fart on a bus. Having a significantly younger sister did not in any way equip me, as it might have, with the capacity to relate to people who struggled to form reasonable sentences. Toddlers were capable of unsettling by deep knowing stares. But Tom was uncomplicated and good at throwing. He asked me questions and received my answers in a quiet, accepting fashion, affording me a certain power and wisdom.

'Can I eat the biscuits even though they've been living on the floor now?'

'Yes.'

That night we ate pizza and listened to Wanda Jackson and played hide and seek and learned about each other.

Carla was from Marseille, which is where the two had met, when Mick went over for a Rugby tour. Mick had grown up here, but he was of Samoan heritage, he told us, combing his lily-white hand through his mousy brown hair. Despite this curiosity, sometime between garlic bread and Coke spiders an unspoken agreement was reached that we were all now to be friends. Over the next few months, we would go over there and eat barbequed snags and play Trivial Pursuit. It was great. It was great for months.

One lazy sun-freckled Saturday arvo, Tom, Georgia and I were bouncing on his backyard trampoline. Mammas and Carla sat watching us from little deckchairs, their faces hidden in giant sunhats and plumes of smoke from their never-ending fags. Our dads fussed over the barbeque, prodding and poking and adding and cooing like proud little pigeons making a nest.

'There's a ghost what lives in my bed with me,' said Tom, as we bounced.

'She's a lady ghost, and she's grown up like Mum.'

'Oh,' I said, 'Is she nice?'

'She gets upset all the time,' said Tom.

Carla sat up and stubbed out her cigarette, lowered her sunglasses, looked at me and said:

'She's recently divorced.'

'Oh.' I said, noting that this indulgence had become curiously adult.

Then Carla looked at Mamma.

'She's grieving because her husband left her recently. She finds a great comfort in sharing Tom's bed.'

We all looked over at Mick, sweating pink over at the barbeque, who, having heard and digested the same information as the rest of us, was completely unmoved.

'Cecelia is harmless though,' he said, pricking all his little sausages. 'For now.'

It's worth noting that my parents had written off people for far less severe crimes than believing in ghosts and expecting us to converse with them about it. But we really liked these guys and their freezer was always full of ice-cream and they had two computers, for Pete's sake. So for now, the ghosts thing was stowed away into the little bundle of curios, along with the fact that Mick said he was ethnically Samoan.

A few months later there was an auction at the house next door to our new friends. A young couple bought it, Katie and Todd. Katie was so pretty and Todd looked like Mel Gibson – before the troubles. They even had a specially bred dog called Melanie, who was smarter than Tom. They also had Foxtel. And they knew how to play Bridge. Katie and Todd were great. So great, in fact, that to this day they are still called Katie and Todd. Soon after they moved in, they fitted nicely into our little gang, and a couple of nights a week the three households would get together for chicken in black-bean sauce and *Seinfeld*. It was one such night during an ad break that Katie made a confession.

Apparently, just after the house was settled, she was wandering around the empty place and decided something about the juju felt off. So she had found a woman in a newspaper advert and paid her, hand over fist, to conduct an exorcism in the house before they moved in.

'I know it's stupid,' she said, 'but I actually felt a lot better afterwards.'

I looked at my parents to see what sort of a response they were calibrating. Could we live with two weird sets of neighbours who believed in ghosts? I couldn't be sure. But it wasn't my parents who I should have been worried about. Turned out, Carla didn't like this revelation at all.

'That explains some things,' said Carla, her eyes locked on the television.

'What do you mean?' said Katie.

'Oh, well I'm not surprised. That's all.'

'We've had lots more ghosts since *you* moved in,' said little Tom from the floor, suggesting that this wasn't the first time a conversation of this nature had taken place in their house. Where an embarrassed laugh and mild chastisement may have been expected, Carla stroked Tom's little head and continued to stare at the scene in Monk's Café.

'You just have to be careful where you put your ghosts, you know?' said Mick, in a way that was intended to make him sound like the voice of reason.

'Oh,' said Katie. 'I had no idea.'

Our whole family was speechless and from our various vantage points slumped over chairs and sofas, all of us with gobs open, we watched, for perhaps the first time, a bristly conversation take place in Annandale that had very little to do with us.

A few weeks later I came home after school to find Carla hanging off our gate. She and Mamma were speaking sombrely, as Carla picked lavender from our garden and tucked it behind her ear. They stopped speaking suddenly when I arrived, and Carla said a curt goodbye and left down the street.

'What was that about?' I asked Mamma as I went inside and threw my backpack on my bed.

'She thinks Katie's dog is shitting on her front lawn.'

'That's weird. Why would Katie let the dog do that?'

'She wouldn't,' said Mamma. 'She definitely wouldn't.'

It was that night, as our family sat around our distressed dining table eating lamb stew, that the immortal phrase was first uttered.

'You know who they are?' said Dad, pulling a big bit of lamb gristle through his teeth. 'They're Madame Guillotine and the Imitation Samoan.'

Dad slurped down the rest of his Chardonnay and slammed the glass on the table. I jumped up to refill it, for this was a momentous occasion.

That was it, we had made up our minds, and now, it was just a waiting game before exile. It could be weeks, it could be months, but a course had now been set.

A few weeks later, Katie came over, very upset. She said some strange things had started happening. Like she hadn't received any mail for a week and the flowers in her front garden were being ripped out few by few, night by night. She had discussed it with Madame Guillotine, who had suggested that it was the work of Cecelia, the divorcee ghost who was sleeping with her three-year-old son.

Immediately we knew that this was the work of Madame Guillotine herself, but Katie didn't want to believe it. After all, Katie and Todd were new villagers, and didn't want to be part of a conspiracy. I could understand that, signing up for *Survivor: Annandale* was a lifetime commitment. Once you are in, you can never get out. For the time being they thought we were mad.

That was of course until one night when Katie saw with her own eyes, from her second storey bedroom window, Madame Guillotine stand on a step ladder, lean right over into her garden with her black shawl billowing in the moonlight and cut down Katie's clothesline with gardening shears.

Katie and Todd came to our house, a mixture of highly amused and terrified. They'd changed their minds, and now needed the help of some hamlet-heavies. Short of returning Madame Guillotine to the pages of the half-formed Anne Radcliffe novel from whence she came, then flushing that novel down the library's toilet, my parents, upon hearing this news, told Katie and Todd to relax, they were on it.

What my parents weren't counting on was that they'd never played *Survivor: Annandale* with someone as completely mental as Madame Guillotine.

They had just commenced the no-eye-contact phase, when Melanie the specially bred dog went missing. Melanie possessed many strange human-like qualities. That, and the fact that she was worth a fucking fortune, caused a serious panic. She showed up in the middle of the night two days later with her butt shaved.

The next day Katie and Todd went straight to their real-estate agent. They said they couldn't take it anymore. My parents begged them to be patient, they explained that they had decades of experience coercing people into moving house, and that if Katie and Todd could just place their trust in them, they could fix everything. But Melanie-napping was their limit, and within the fortnight the house had been put on the market and a few weeks after that, Katie and Todd were gone.

A dark mortification filled our house. For the first time ever, someone had out-played my parents at *Survivor: Annandale*. Not only had their twenty-year reign of being the only people awful enough to compel neighbours to actually move come to an end, but the only actual friends they had left on the street had been scratched out by their enemies.

They knew they'd have to upscale, think outside the box, maybe consult their mate Charlie who was at that time facing court for squirting superglue into the keyhole of a hardware store's front door. He told the court that this was because they sold spray-paint and he considered himself to be a great protector of the inner west against graffiti.

They'd barely hatched any semblance of a plan with Charlie when one afternoon a bag of old dog shit showed up in our mailbox.

That night Mamma made us all spaghetti and meatballs. She gave us each a kiss on the forehead, picked up the bag of dog shit and said she'd be back in fifteen minutes.

Mamma never told me exactly what happened.

'I was very nice,' she said, while casually picking dog shit and what could have been hair out of her fingernails.

The house was on the market two weeks later.

When moving day came, my parents geared up for one final Fuck You. Was it elegant? No. Effective? A little. They rose early got in Crap Car (our family's trusty travelling steed) and parked it at an angle so it took up the two available spaces out the front of Madame Guillotine and the Imitation Samoan's house. When the removalist truck, once again, wound its way into the heart of the little village it had to park a bit further away than would have been desirable. It was of little consequence that my parents couldn't use their own car for the weekend. Whatever impact was suffered by having to walk further than necessary, whatever extra time and cost that added to the move, that and the fact that for an entire weekend Madame Guillotine and the

Imitation Samoan had to stare at my parents' awful disintegrating car, was surely worth it.

And the years passed, and the cycle continued. More recently a little middle-aged man moved into the neighbourhood. Within a year he had somehow transformed his beautiful federation cottage into what looked like a lunchbox made from concrete, and not in a Frank Gehry way. My parents hated this man, but sort of kept him round like a fly in a web, teasing and poking but not letting natural selection take its course. Dad recently called me to say that someone had, with the engraving skills of a delicate monk, etched the word 'cunt' on the passenger door of the man's brand new Lexus.

'And it wasn't even me!' he said, proudly. 'See Zoë, that's how much of a cunt he is, *other people* think he's a cunt.'

This was a very special day. Mamma and Dad weren't getting any younger after all, and they were only too pleased to know that their torch had been passed to a new generation. A silent vigilante-cum-Banksy who would carry *Survivor: Annandale* into the future, and my parents could retire undefeated.

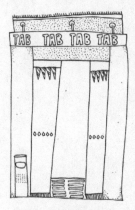

The Marron

The Marron

O ne evening at the age of ten, Georgia had been assigned hunting and gathering duties. Up until I finished Year Six, Mamma had insisted on walking me to school in the mornings and picking me up in the afternoons. This was a school that could be seen perfectly well from the vantage point of our house. She also used to watch me playing in the park, from the window in the lounge room, and would make me come inside hours before any of my comrades were summoned for dinner. Somewhat predictably Georgia's world was a lot more relaxed than mine, and, at the age of ten she was deemed perfectly capable of the financial and physical responsibilities involved in a solo trip to the fish-and chip-shop. I was sixteen at the time, and wading through an entirely new swamp of Mamma's overprotective tendencies. At any rate, the unfairness was not lost on me, and out of pettiness I insisted on going with her. Whilst it promised no particular joy to me, minimising Georgia's freedom was a little pleasure unto itself. And it was on this particular adventure that Georgia and I happened upon a shellfish walking down the street.

Amongst the evening's take-away diners, potential trivia guests lolling into the pub, and the late night patients off to see the Johnston Street doctor with varying imagined and real middle-class diseases, amongst them all, and Georgia and me, walking down the street was a shiny black shellfish.

The shellfish was a handsome creature with significant black pincers stretching out in front of it. It walked with a sense of purpose, as though it should have been carrying a miniature top hat and cane.

Having no precedent for what to do when coming upon a shellfish in Annandale, Georgia decided she wanted to follow it. We strolled behind this thing, and began to wonder where its slow yet undeviating journey was heading.

Perhaps the creature had escaped from the shopping bag of an old lady who'd recently been to the fish markets. It could have just been a favourite pet of a child, a little boy riddled with allergies but resistant to pincer stabbings, and maybe it had seized the opportunity of an open cage and fled into the blissful sunlight of the rest of its life.

But there was something about its elegant metronomic gait that made it look more like it was heading to a regular appointment. That and the fact, when it came to a corner, instead of stepping out into the traffic, it made a purposeful right-hand turn.

Perhaps it was off to see the minister at the Hunter Baillie Church, or maybe it was heading east to the Glebe Town Hall for the annual shellfish moot, Port Jackson chapter. It's possible the creature had recently read some Kerouac and was testing its aptitude for adventure. Maybe the shellfish had just told its wife and son that it was stepping out for a packet of fags and a carton of milk, never to return to the stifling domesticity it must own a part in creating. Maybe if we had had the presence of mind to ask it to grant three wishes, we would know by now. The creature could have been an ASIO spy in the best and most dangerous of disguises. Maybe it was in search of a soapbox onto which it would climb to protest about Council plans to allow more high density apartment blocks to be built in the old Children's Hospital or the lack of shellfish crossing signs on Trafalgar Street. We could have been bearing witness to the stupidest of all the Biblical plagues or perhaps we were simply trapped in a lesser known Salvador Dali painting. Either that, or the shellfish was simply heading to the bus stop on Booth Street, to catch the 370 back to the sea.

While we were trying to work out what was going on, we heard a car door slam shut, just next to us. A tall, suited man with oily hair and little eyes had stepped out of his shiny black car.

'Is that your marron?' he said, pointing to our new friend.

'Yes,' said Georgia.

'No,' I said at the same time. The tall man bent down and stroked the back of the creature with his long index finger.

'Do you know what you're dealing with here?'

'Yes,' said Georgia.

'This is a *marron*. A *marron*.' he said.

'I *know*,' said Georgia. She didn't.

'What are you going to do with it?'

Georgia looked at her new friend, and then out onto the gentrified wasteland, and then to me for a rare moment of sisterly guidance. I shrugged, not really giving a shit.

'I'd be delighted to take it home,' he said, smiling so that his little eyes all but disappeared into his face. Georgia paused.

'I suppose,' she said.

'Thank you,' he said, and smiled.

The man picked up the marron and started walking to his car.

'My kids will think it's chicken.' he said as he closed the door.

The engine revved and Georgia, horrified, ran towards the window.

The man was holding the creature up to it to say goodbye. It scratched its pincers at her as if to say 'Why?'

We came home that day with just three bags of fish and chips and a chocolate bar for Georgia. Years of bearing witness to countless strange and unholy maritime-related deaths in our fishtank had hardened me to the harsh realities of the wild, but Georgia was a mere babe in this regard, and the culinary fate of this strange little friend she had met walking down the street weighed heavily on her mind.

To this day, Georgia remains a vegetarian. And though she can recite a catalogue of ethical reasons informing her lifestyle choice, I'm pretty sure it's a simple matter of crustacean-trauma.

Hats

One evening Dad came out of the bathroom making a guttural sound from his deepest insides. He staggered into the hallway and spat out a foamy spray of white stuff, splattering all over Mamma's 'Purple Flowers on Vine' painting that she had made in art class, and giving it a slightly enhanced sense of Impressionism. We thought he was dying.

It turned out, he explained, after gouging the gunk out of his mouth with his fingers and then washing it down with two half-bottles of Chardonnay, that he had brushed his teeth with tinea cream by mistake.

On a different evening Dad was asking Georgia how come if she was a vegetarian she sometimes drank soy milk.

There were a few things about this that Little Georgia and I did not understand. Firstly, soy milk *is* the milk that vegans drank, we said. Secondly, Little Georgia isn't a vegan, she is a vegetarian so she can drink any type of milk.

'But soy milk…comes from a soy,' said Dad.

'What do you mean by…"a soy"?' Little Georgia asked.

'You know…' said Dad, and then he held his hands to the side of his face, splayed out his fingers and made a sort of hissing sound, doing an impression of whatever kind of ghastly animal he thinks a 'soy' is.

Dad denies that this ever happened, but I remember it and Little Georgia remembers it and Dad had drunk two half-bottles of Chardonnay so what he doesn't remember doesn't count.

I think he had probably partaken of his favourite drink when he took me and Little Georgia out on a sail boat when we were on a holiday at a resort in Cairns. The boat sat in a merry line of boats for the taking, all sitting on the edge of a very placid, manmade lagoon. We spun in circles of pointless whimsy through the lagoon as Dad had no idea how to use a sailboat, watched on by cheerful holiday makers on banana chairs in the Queensland sun. After a fashion, all the people started screaming, because they realised, far quicker than Dad, that in spite of the seemingly certain safety of this situation, we were about to have a boat accident. It turned out, we realised long after everyone else, that we were about to crash into the rocky walled edge of the lagoon. Dad's strategy in this situation, rather than attempting to change course, was to jump out of the boat, in his socks and leather slippers, and stand between it and the rocky wall. Dad had decided that he cared much more about not paying for boat repairs than he did about his own body, and thus he fashioned himself as a sort of human buffer. Should his endeavour have failed, he'd hoped his life insurance would at least pay for the damages.

I was much relieved that Dad didn't die that day. After all, there is no biopic for the man who is killed by a boat that is so rudimentary children are allowed to operate it in what is essentially a swimming pool.

The results were mixed. We were deeply embarrassed which was a minus. And we definitely did damage the boat, quite a lot, but beyond that there were no repercussions. Apparently the resort that had a 'boats for any idiot' policy wasn't ready for the lawsuit and bad press that might come if they asked Dad to pay for it.

But sometimes Dad can be quite manly. For example, he keeps a shabby-chic-ed axe handle under the bed to scare off intruders. More than once, Mamma and Georgia and I have stood on the porch watching Dad race down the street in his underpants brandishing the weapon at confused burglars.

Dad is a little bit of a goose. And like most geese flying south for winter or being freezer packed for Christmas dinner, he likes rituals. And there is one ritual Dad has, which, in spite of some of his other exhibitions, everyone follows with reverence and grace.

It's called Hats.

There are conditions that need to be apparent for Hats. They include, and are exhaustively, having other people in our house who are not in our family, who have never played Hats before.

Hats starts in The Hat Room. As far as I can tell, there are only three types of people who have a Hat Room. Queens, mad people, and people whose children have recently moved out of home.

In the Hat Room there is a large wooden Hat Rack for all the Hats. Other notable items in the Hat Room include a dartboard, that Dad uses to play Cricket Darts with people who are not in the family, who have never played Cricket Darts before. Cricket Darts is a game he invented which doesn't make sense to any humans, except him. There is also a CD player of which Dad is very proud. On the mantelpiece there are ointments for rashes and keys with no purpose. There is also a single bed, which is the perfect size for falling asleep on by accident. There is a big piece of cardboard above the Hat Rack. I brought it home when I was the Person Of The Week in Year One. When you're the Person Of The Week in Year One, Ms Miranda asks everyone in the class to think of things you're really good at and then she writes them on a piece of cardboard and then you take the cardboard home. Dad has kept it because it says 'Zoë Is An Excellent Silent Reader'. Dad doesn't doubt the meritocracy of the Person Of The Week system or my skills as a silent reader. He merely queries *how* they *knew* I was an Excellent Silent Reader and it remains on the wall like an impenetrable proverb, something to consider in times of exasperation. But nary an item is so important as the Hats. There is a Panama hat and a pork-pie one too. There's a twirly-whirly, propeller-enhanced baseball cap and a plastic cowboy hat with two beer holders and gangly rotting straws attached. There's Santa's Elf, Akubra and Greek fisherman's hats. A beanie, a bowler and a bucket hat. A war helmet with goggles, a Balinese hat with bells, a hard hat, a beret, a shower cap and a fez.

Hats starts when Dad says 'It's Time for Hats.' Then he bids people attend him to the Hat Room where he bestows upon everyone's head a hat of his choosing. Then he presses play on the CD player and everyone dances to whatever is inside the CD player for the duration of one song. Then everyone resumes his or her prior activity, sweaty and with Hat.

Then people subtly try to remove the hats from their heads, but this makes Dad mad, so they put them back on. Then they leave their hats on until Dad has had enough half-bottles of Chardonnay to forget he ever started Hats.

The Birds

A week before my fifteenth birthday a man named Dale came to our front door. Dale was just one of those middle-aged men who existed in Annandale. Nobody knew from whence he came or what comprised his days, or how he slept at night. Or at least I didn't. Dale was wet and red about all the important parts of his face and his person was accompanied by a chakra of bin juice. The rivets in his knuckles were puttied over with historical grime and a crescent moon of hairy belly peeked through the bottom of his Newtown Jets jersey. He was the kind of adult who made me swear I would never, ever be one. He held a Diet Coke in one hand and a black wire cage in the other. In the cage there was a little plastic gum tree, a suspended golden bell, two budgies and a smattering of silvery-white shit all over the bars of the cage and slopping down onto the newspaper that covered the base.

'Delivery!' he yelled, clumping down our hallway, and homing the cage and its contents on the end of our *distressed* white dining-room table. These formative teen years of mine will be remembered as the Age of Shabby-chic. For the uninitiated, shabby-chic: (pronounced 'sheek') is a form of interior design where furniture and furnishings are either purchased or rendered after purchase to look terrible. All the bits of furniture in our house were subjected to the same cruelty. Once they had been bargained away from a garage sale they went straight to the garden for a brutal shabby-chic-ing. Then they returned to the house, members of the master race. Dining table (distressed), Mamma's Dresser (distressed), Doors (distressed), Legs of Barbeque (distressed). Even our family weapon, an axe handle, was painted the streaky white of the alleged fashion.

Georgia and I came out to meet the bird-hostages, one for each of us. We had been expecting them.

'These birds is for the little birds!' said Dale, then he laughed so hard at his attempted joke I thought he might faint.

Georgia named hers Crystal, and I, duty-bound to the rules of matchy-matchy, named mine Pearl. She had a somewhat disfiguring overgrown beak, my Pearl, a lumpy sculpture, which meandered aimlessly around her greenish, feathered head. Having a significant overbite myself, I felt as though Pearl and I possessed the sympatico to develop a true connection. Where I slept with a metal plate, Pearl's situation was to be remedied, according to Dale, by trimming the thing regularly with nail scissors. Pearl was unmoved by our shared plight, and instead of compliantly jutting her monster-beak through the cage when I would approach her, scissors in hand, she would shriek and lacerate my fingers with her ghastly snaggle-pecker and claws, as though deep in the throes of ice-induced mania.

One morning, a few months later, I awoke from a series of fetid, sweaty dreams, clammy and sick to my stomach. A pungent, chemical musk permeated the house. It turned out the neighbours had called in the termite man. And while they had sensibly removed themselves from ground zero, enjoying a spot of Foxtel at the Medina, the toxic gases had seeped under their house, drifted eastward, and oozed up through our floorboards.

Pearl and Crystal were discovered by Dad, motionless at the bottom of their shit-splattered cage. He broke the news to us, gently.

'Girls, I have to tell you something. Come and sit down,' he said, bidding us to settle either side of him on the distressed settee.

'Pearl and Crystal have gone to heaven.'

Georgia was essentially indifferent. I was relieved, although I had developed a deep mistrust of those terrible flying things with their I-can-see-you-all-the-time eyes and their demonic heads that can spin almost completely around. This wasn't such a problem for a long time. Being whatever the antithesis of an outdoors-woman is, it was extremely rare that I had to face this particular orthinological uneasiness. That was until many years later, when I had essentially failed at life.

With an unspeakable credit-card debt and a seven-year hangover, a decided lack of personal agency, an extra six kilos and a short dissertation on the effects of eating all one's main meals from the convenience store, at twenty-eight I moved back into to my parents' distressed kingdom in Annandale.

The rusty slippery slide in the park next door with its exposed nails that used to punish the buttocks of any child not equipped with agricultural-grade denim jeans, is now a twirly plastic space machine engineered with soft corners and flashing lights. The Rottweilers mauling each other to death and pissing on a middle-aged woman asleep in the sun with sticky gin and her tongue lolling out of her mouth which is buzzing with flies, are now fluffy white labradoodles, made in a lab, tethered to women who wear well-on-trend activewear and push babies who can read on swings that have seatbelts. The bushland with passages at White's Creek Park carved out by pre-teen-made molotovish cocktails, are now Council-made wetlands where kids draw pictures of frogs and don't ever touch them and compare notes for the big anti-bullying assignment instead of chilling out on couches dragged across from the tip in the cindery blown-up bush passages, watching battery-operated TVs and bonging out, like the eleven year olds of yore.

And sometime in the sunset of some year in the middle of the ten or so years since I left this place and came back, my parents decided to replace me and Georgia with eight rainbow lorikeets, two magpies and fifty pigeons.

The kids at the wetlands could tell my parents that you don't feed the birds. But they do feed the birds. Eight-dollar loaves of sourdough and miche made by a celebrity baker from Masterchef and English muffins. They have nails on the back fence for the birds to feed from. They favour the birds in an unmovable hierarchy based mainly on colour, in a similar fashion to how they seem to feel about the people that run and have run the ailing corner shop across the road. Obviously the rainbow lorikeets are the best because they're the most colourful, then the magpies cause they're the most big, and all the pigeons who all look the same as each other can go fuck themselves or face the contents of an overful ashtray flung by my mother's bangle-jangling wrist right at their stupid sameyness.

I don't like the wetlands and I don't like the way my Dad coos to a bird on his hand in the garden as it eats a warm, buttery scone.

But recently a line was crossed, an embargo was

violated, an umbilical cord severed, a beachside town submerged forever. Something irrevocably happened when one morning I walked into the kitchen and heard a tapping.

In the kitchen was a magpie, tapping his beak into the hardwood floor.

Feed me you bitch. Feed me somethin' special.

I waved my hand to shoo it away and in instinct-abandon it flew at my face and said:

Feed me you bitch. This magpie be hungry, so does its baby and its baby mummy.

The toaster popped and the bird settled on the bench and I fed it a slice of warm crusty bread.

That's it bitch. You get how this works, this be my joint now and if you want to stay here you better get better with that bread and butter.

It said this with its mouth full and flew out the door, leaving a legacy of lethal beak marks all over the floor.

And Mamma and Dad came out and observed the scene.

Zoë! What have you done? What the hell have you done?

And Dad rushed out and cooed the magpie better with a handful of bagel chips from the deli and the hideous bird sat on Mamma's shoulder and shat down her dress, giving her that distressed look she loves so dear.

'Look what you've done! You can't feed native Australian birds bloody wondershite! It gives them irritable bowel syndrome!'

But now the birds come into the house, every day and

they flap on the bench and tap at the bread they feel like that day and if you screw their order they'll peck at your face and if you get it right they'll pay you in bird shit.

And I think back to that rusty slide where I once stood at three years old and asked my daddy to get me the moon and he said 'Sure baby girl, anything for you.'

But apparently if you leave your parents empty-nesters they'll take it both personally and literally and replace you with birds.

Phylly

Phylly is about four-and-a-half-feet tall and built like a very small but extremely competent ox. She currently holds court in a suburb many kilometres away from Annandale, but she was born on a little island in Greece called Syros, known for its enduring medieval qualities. I honestly have no idea how long Phylly has been on Planet Earth. Her extreme agility, excellent skin and confidence with the public transport system sit at odds with her other-worldly qualities and traditional customs.

Phylly had been coming to clean our house once a fortnight since I was about ten. She was by no means the first cleaner we had, but she was the best. She was also the most Greek, which was very important. This meant that as well as reliably arriving with a cloth bag full of homegrown tomatoes, freshly baked *kourabiethes* and Windex, Phylly could find anything in our house. From an inexplicably misplaced toaster wedged under the couch to a solitary lost diamond stud, dancing precariously on the bathroom drain. If we had lost it, she could find it. Phylly cleaned things we didn't know needed cleaning, like the inside of the linen cupboard doors, the underside of the mantelpieces and the bases of the lamps. Very quickly she became the beating heart of our house. This was because we loved her deeply, and also because if she stopped cleaning our muck and providing us with food, we probably would have died. Eventually, when she was about one hundred and sixty Phylly fired *us*, but from when I was ten through to about twenty-six, she would come over to our house once a fortnight to exorcise our filth demons, ply us with food and impart mystifying advice.

There was really only one thing I resented about Phylly. And that was Tuesday nights, when, after dinner, we all had to up stumps and 'Phylly the house'. This meant cleaning it. Just like the Hoover, Phylly was so good, she had become a verb and we had to Phylly the house before Phylly came over to Phylly it better. I assume this had something to do with shame.

I loved Phylly a lot because she always brought me exotic presents, like an orange hand-towel with rabbit ears dangling pointlessly off one end or a baseball cap that said 'Captain Princess' on the front in pink lettering with a sparkly gold hair scrunchie attached to it at the back. I loved her because she never forgot our Greek name days, even though we always did. And I loved her not least of all because she called Parramatta Road, *Kalamata* Road. And she said it a lot, because it was a big part of her multi-bus adventure from wherever she came from to Annandale. 'Oh, Zoë, so much traffic on Kalamata Road today.'

I loved Phylly even though she thought I was fat. I knew this because she told me all the time.

'Zoëëëëëëë,' she'd say, clicking her tongue and shaking her head, tears almost springing into her eyes, 'you put on so much the weight, plee, *pleeeee,* telephonay they Weight Jenny Watchy,' she would say, frequently, while simultaneously placing a wobbly selection of home-made Greek sweets on my desk with a little fork. 'Zoëëëëëëë you eat this now. It will make you smarts,' she'd say afterwards, winking, confusingly.

There was the odd occasion, rare as hen's teeth, when Phylly would walk into our house, look me up and down and decide that I had actually lost some weight. When this happened, she'd say, 'Zoëëëëëëë, you lose so much the weight! *Pleeeee, pleeeee* donay put it back on!'

One day when I was about sixteen, Phylly dobbed on me for eating sweets. She told Mamma, gravely, that she had found *four* chocolate wrappers in my room. Somehow she had missed the bong. Either that, or, true to form, her chief concern was doing what she could, once a fortnight, to assist the community project of making sure Zoë did not get any fatter.

Phylly wasn't the only person in my life who is irrationally concerned about how much physical space my form takes up in the world. My relationship with my Papou has essentially been reduced to him walking into our house on Christmas day, looking at me and bursting into tears. Every year, I think he is crying because he is so elated to see me. Until he says, through his wet whimpers, 'Zoë, you're so fat!'

The most annoying thing about this is that my Papou is roughly the shape and size of a bungalow.

One Christmas, a few years ago, I took leave of my repressed emotions and decided to respond.

'Zoë, you're so fat!'

'Papou. Get fucked.' The words were out of my mouth and in the ears of my entire extended family before I realised what I had said.

'What?' he said, horrified.

'I said, Papou. Get fucked.'

I wasn't sure how this was going to go down with the clan who were all standing around our dining room. It was entirely possible for a Christmas to deteriorate into a little bickering later in the proceedings, but this was first thing in the morning. No one even had lipstick on their teeth yet. I looked at Yia Yia, the Leader of the Pack. The one whose response would dictate the response of all others. She was sitting on a chair next to a little plate of prawns. And she was smiling. She gestured for me to come over, pulled out her little leather purse, prised open its gold clasp with her impossibly long fingernails and pulled out a wad of cash. She pressed one-hundred dollars into my hand.

From my very small observational study that I undertook when I was three years old, the problem of being simultaneously called fat and being force-fed is much worse in actual Greece. Mamma and Dad and I were staying in a little block of flats, right on the sea, on a tiny island called Karystos. In the flat next door to ours lived Christina and her Yia Yia. Christina had cellulite and Christina was also three years old, like me. 'Christina, she does not eat!' the Yia Yia would say, while mashing up *koulourakia* biscuits into her granddaughter's bottle of milk. Every day, she'd take Christina to the park for exercise, where she'd place the kid on the swing, give her an almighty push and then stand in front of her with a giant bowl of octopus salad. Every time Christina would swing forward, her Yia Yia would shove a ladle of octopus and feta and oily limp lettuce in her mouth. Occasionally I would be left in the loving company of Christina and her Yia Yia where I would have to endure the same confusing torture. I also couldn't really walk more than a few metres in any direction on the island without being pummelled with ingestibles. I had to get three fillings before I left Greece, and the only thing

I can remember how to say is '*Ochi pagoto,*' which means 'No ice-cream', a phrase I had to deploy ten times a day. I was also traumatised by a man called Vangelli who said 'Zoë, one night when you asleep, I'm gonna come into your room, I'm gonna cut off your hair, I'm gonna give it to my son.' Apparently he meant well.

Anyway, Phylly wasn't quite that bad. And she had lots of amazing other qualities. I knew Phylly was special and confusing but we had obviously skimmed over the part on her resume about her experience with miracles.

One day, after a great many years of long service, our dishwasher packed in. The dishwasher guy came round. He laughed at our dishwasher, that he decreed to be twenty years old and dead. Vital wires which were responsible for its capacity to turn on had fizzled and snapped in half. It was over. And like so many other fixed appliances that gave out in our house, it sat there, a steel corpse, for over a year. We'd try it out once every few months, to see if it had come to its senses, but it remained, as all dead things tend to, unable to wash dishes.

One day Phylly came over with a little bottle of holy water from the Greek church.

'I put little bit of basil inside the bottle for extra good luck,' she said.

My mother looked at the bottle. 'Thank you, Phylly,' she said as she put it in the pantry.

'Holy water. You just use little sprinkle to fix things.'

Mamma isn't particularly religious, but she does believe in homeopathy. That afternoon, when Phylly set off into the away-from-Annandale sun, Mamma experienced a moment of insanity. She went to the pantry, picked up the holy water, sprinkled a little bit of it into the dishwasher, put in a dirty coffee cup and an ashtray and pressed the 'wash' button. Nothing happened. She turned to walk outside for a fag and she heard a murmur. Then a splutter. Then a beautiful hum. She spun around. A green light had come on the dishwasher and the great machine had returned from the dead. Mamma started screaming, and we all ran into the kitchen.

'It fucking works!' she screamed.

The next week when Phylly came round, Mamma told her what had happened.

'Why you surprise? Holy water. It's for fixings,' she said, and then stuffed her skirt into her knickers, grabbed a bottle of Exit Mould and climbed into the bath.

The dishwasher continued to work for another three years, and Phylly got a healthy raise.

Phylly was with me all the way through puberty, steadily tracking my progress as I slowly flabbed out and pimplified, much to her dismay. One day in that largely forgettable period between finishing school and renting my own place, I came home to find quite a sight. It took me a little while to put my finger on what was wrong, but something about my room looked awry. Then I saw it.

It was atop my mantelpiece. The arrangement looked a little something like this: candle, candle, oil burner, candle, vibrator, candle, ornament, candle. In amongst the delicately dusted candles and ornaments, all perfectly spaced one inch apart, was my pink vibrator, or Pinky the First as he would later come to be known. I had never truly appreciated his iridescence before then, as I only dealt with him in the shameful dark. But there he was, reliably erect and situated between a candle shaped like Mozart and a figurine of a cat on its hind legs — either of which could have served as a suitable replacement for the vibrator proper, should I ever lose it, I thought, as I tried to process what had happened.

Evidently, Phylly had cleaned my room, found the vibrator under my bed, *cleaned it* and put it on my mantelpiece. There were two explanations: either she thought it was an ornament, or she thought it was a vibrator. If she thought it was an ornament, I should probably buy her a vibrator. But, *if* she thought it was a vibrator, and she shined it up like a diamond and then put it on my mantelpiece, then she may have been a sort of sociopathic sex-pest in lovely old Greek lady's clothing. I still don't know which one was the case, because all Phylly and I ever talked about was how fat I was, and I wanted to keep things simple, as I had enough complicated relationships in my life.

I couldn't decide what was more upsetting, the fact that

Phylly had put my vibrator on the mantlepiece, or the fact that just a few hours before, Phylly was sitting on my bed with a dust cloth and a bottle of Windex putting her elbow grease to work on my vibrator. So I brought Mamma into the room for a second opinion. Mamma was mortified. She told me to make sure I hid it extremely well in the future.

The next week, I totally forgot to put the vibrator in a locker at Central Station or whatever Mamma wanted me to do. This time I came home to find that Phylly had created a sort of sculpture on my desk. It went roughly: *Developmental Psychology For Beginners* textbook, *A Room of One's Own* by Virginia Woolf, French dictionary, TV Guide, Donna Hay cookbook, vibrator. Did she think it was a bookmark? Or perhaps a night-light?

I was sitting in my room staring at the weird Tetris ensemble of books and vibrator, all arranged with the delicate intent of a naïve and expert cleaner or the delicate intent of an experienced and expert sex maniac. Phylly knocked on the door.

'Zoë,' she said. 'I'm not scared of you.'

'Sorry Phylly?'

'I said. Zoë. I'm not scared of you.'

Was she talking about my vibrator?

'You go to university. You do study. I'm not scared of you, you going to be okay.'

'Oh, you're not worried about me, is that what you mean?'

'Yes. That is what I mean.'

But there was just something in her tone that suggested it wasn't just ESL at play. Like maybe the fact that she knew I had a vibrator and that she was putting it in weird places to mess with my mind.

Either that or there was something more prophetic at work. Perhaps Phylly knew that I would be faced with challenges in my near future. Challenges for which I would be prepared because my cleaner had cleaned my vibrator.

Maybe she looked into her crystal ball and saw me in my share house, aged twenty, when Dad would come over to fix my wardrobe.

I had essentially mastered living out of home. Detergent, bread, throwing electricity bills in the recycling bin and having my Dad on speed dial for when I couldn't turn off a smoke alarm or a door fell off my overflowing wardrobe. He came over with a handful of screws and a can of WD40. After he finished his task, he came into the lounge room, where I was drinking beer with my friends, wiped sweat of his face and announced to the general assembly in his Welsh accent, 'You wouldn't believe what I found under Zoë's bed.'

'Stop, Dad.'

'Various items, in varying states of decay.'

There was, unfortunately, no mistaking exactly what my Dad meant. Especially when he went on to elaborate.

'Some in boxes, others gathering dust.'

My friends looked at me, and I looked to the sky and thanked Phylly for giving me some preparatory experience.

Night of the Possums

I have a secret friend. And that friend is a Possum.

A superior friend to Princess Jade the slug who faded when I upgraded her house from a tea strainer to a Tupperware container.

Do you want a bite of my Space Food Stick, Little Possum?

Mamma buys them at Coles because if she doesn't Little Georgia bashes her head on the floor until Mamma can't take it anymore and people look at her like someone who commits child harm and they look at me the way you look at someone with a broken arm.

So listen, I can only feed you after Dad passes out on the sofa and Mamma goes and pretends to work on the computer otherwise I'll get busted and then there'll be no more custard tarts or sachets of McDonald's mustard or anything.

And night after night I'll sneak out and feed you and feed you and feed you and feed you and feed you and feed you. Aeroplane jelly and pizza pockets and pizza rounders and tinned peaches and Cadbury Favourites and pikelets and trifle and Dunkaroos and Starburst fruit chews and fruit loaf and meatloaf and pea and ham soup and fruit loops and Iced Vovos and chocolate Yogos and peppermint Freddos and my hands will get scratchy and bleedy and I think maybe I love you.

And I keep our love a secret because I'm not supposed to feed you. I'm not supposed to have any fun. Isn't that right Mamma?

And I'll stop caring about things a bit like how shit school is and how I wish I didn't have tits yet.

And I'll stop caring so much that I open the fridge and the pantry at the same time and I fill a plastic bag with my desperation to please you and everything edible. Everything you could possibly dream of in your dreamy, furry head.

And Mamma takes a break from pretending to work on the computer and wanders into the kitchen and wonders where is the chocolate éclair she just bought? She just bought it and now it's gone. And for that matter where is the bread? She swears there were oranges and hard-boiled sweets and soft-boiled eggs and pink cured meats. And she turns on the outside light and sees in the garden the half eaten packets and bits and bites and pieces of everything that seems to be missing from her kitchen.

And Mamma asks me, 'Have you been feeding possums, like you know you're not allowed to?'

'Mamma. It could have been anyone. You can't just blame me because it's easy. It could have been Dad or Little Georgia or a big scary robber who could be in the house right now *you cow*.'

'There's chocolate éclair in your hair, Zoë. Go to your room.'

'Fine. I like my room anyway.'

No I don't.

I'm going to redecorate my room.

Yeah…yeah, I hate this chair it can go there. And this can go here and that can go there and this can go here and that stable table can get lost and if I keep going like this I'll probably be paralysed and Mamma will feel like a bloody idiot.

And Mamma will knock on the door.

'What do you want from me? I'm busy. I didn't slam a door. I didn't.'

And I open the door, just a crack, bearing its weight so it appears to be straight and not sixty per cent off its hinges. It's a really old door, in fact it was always like that I'm sure.

Mamma, a man could have climbed through my window because it doesn't lock and he could be in here right now beating me across the face with a hammer. I could be beaten to death on the floor and all you care about is your precious door. You care more about the door than you do about me. It's not phooey it's plain to see. Don't call me names! What kind of a Mamma calls their kid names? The same kind of Mamma who won't fix a lock on the bedroom window of their first born. Goodbye.

Slam. And I'll slam the door.

And my stupid demented contented family will be watching telly and eating ice-cream and jelly without me.

And I'll go to bed and close my eyes and feel so so so so so so so so so sorry for myself.

And I'll try to think of things that make me happy. Really, really wanting Little Georgia (before she was born). Practicing trying on my school uniform. My pen licence. Saying a long word for the first time with casual accuracy. What's going on with that coconut? Is it *desiccated*? French knitting. Acrostic poems. Contacting exercise books. Forbidden toiletries like pink ointments with gold labels and loofahs and wax and pumice stones and exfoliants and epilators and emulsifiers and tongue scrapers and gauze and royal jelly and leave-in conditioner.

And then from within the deep self-interested oneness of dreaming confusing feelings, confusing feelings that must be felt quietly and alone so as to keep intact that most private, singular moan, that moan that can never be corrupted by the implied presence of a person disgusted at those repulsive thoughts, thoughts so unwholesome no one has ever thought them before.

And then in the middle of my pre-teen most private dream…

'There's something on my face! There's something on my face!'

And I'll swipe at the claws on my face and something hisses and I scream.

'Turn on the light! Turn on the light!'

And Dad is standing there holding a lit candle and an axe handle.

And we watch the last of the possums disappear up the chimney.

The last but two the last but two! Dad! Go, go, go!

The window! The window! And Dad drops what he's holding and they scratch at his face as he hurls them by their tails out the open window.

And then fuck! The candle! He stamps his feet on the flaming TV guide on the floor.

And then fuck! He's not wearing shoes.

And then in the light everything that was dark is bright. Necklaces and bracelets disembeaded like rainbow vomit, books with their spines snapped, stamp collection re-stamped with possum shit, and possum shit in every skirting-bordered corner, troll dolls beheaded, cushions

111

with their cotton woolly hearts bursting out of their broken possum shitty chests.

And then from the hallway: 'Possums have been in the house,' says Mamma.

No shit Mamma.

'A hat has fallen off the hat-stand and there are pellets of poo in my Jimmy Choos, good God!' she says as she enters my room and sees me out of the covers, Dad nursing his foot and all the chimney soot and possum shit and broken everything.

'This is your fault Zoë.'

And in runs Little Georgia screaming and holding the bodyless head of a china doll with possum shit where its eyes once were.

'Zoë, take Little Georgia into the bathroom and lock it. That will be the Panic Room. Go.'

And I take Little Georgia by the hand down the hall and a possum jumps off the bookshelf and lands like a cat and hisses as it pisses on our feet.

Mamma runs out with a big broom and sweeps the possum into my room.

'Why is it going in my room?'

'Quarantine. Now go to the Panic Room. Go!'

Sitting on the bathroom floor we hear Mamma yell at Dad to lock every window and door and we hear the moving of furniture up against every potentially penetrable opening in the house.

And then scuttles and scratches and hisses and whacks.

They're still in the house and there's no way out and four curly hands poke their way through the little gap between door and floor in the Panic Room and then the sounds of a boot and a shovel and a scream and the curly hands are gone for now.

And Mamma says to open the door just a crack and to hold Little Georgia back and I do and with bloodied hands she passes me two bowls of cornflakes and spoons and her jewellery box then closes the door and then scuffles and shuffles and Mamma starts jumping and screaming at Dad.

'Don't fucking stare! Get it out of my hair!'

Little Georgia sits on the toilet, blinking wildly and eating her cornflakes, and eating her hair which is basting in cornflakes.

I wonder if possums have rabies or scabies or syphilis. Probably, I think as I hear Mamma fending possums away with a can of olive oil spray.

We eat our cornflakes and try on Mamma's jewellery as the bathroom gets colder and the night gets older and stranger.

Little Georgia, signet- and wedding-ringed with worry-beaded gypsy crown makes a castle of toilet rolls and bottles of Dettol and starts scratching her arms and yelling out to Mamma, 'Zoë's hitting me with a big stick,' even though I'm not. But Mamma, who's gone mad outside as she sprays possums away with a can of whipped cream, either doesn't hear or care so when Little Georgia's larynx is red raw she pours the Dettol around the castle and makes a moat for a keg of soap boat which floats for a moment and then settles soggy near the drain.

I think I hear the sound of an axe handle swoop at a possum near a light and miss the possum and hit the light and I think I hear bare feet stepping on glass but so much time has passed we're getting fast to the arse end of the night so I can't be sure what I'm hearing. And I don't think I've been up this late ever and the ancient night has gotten the better of gypsy Little Georgia who has broken down her castle with a toilet brush tomahawk and perches on the sink eating talcum powder and I'm so tired but she can't die on my watch so I tie her to the toilet with a towel and we play I spy.

Towel, toilet, toe-nail scissors, toothbrush, tampons, tablets, teatree oil, Tamiflu, tinea cream, tapeworm pills, typhoid ointment, toxic-shock-syndrome patches, tuberculosis tonic, tetanus shot.

And in the feverish micro-sleeping sunrise we vaguely hear what might be the sound of Dad driving a long way away with a boot full of possums.

And somehow through some unremembered great effort I confuse myself all the way back to bed and sleep all the long school day long. And everything is wrong all through the day's dreams. A sunflower is a power drill and a daisy chain is a guillotine and there is my friend, the possum, the size of an ocean liner and he sits wide legged on a sea of meringue with a giant bib and eats Dad and his axe handle and Little Georgia in her toilet-roll castle and Mamma holding a can of olive oil spray who says as the foul black teeth chew her in half, 'This is *your* fault Zoë.'

And possums can go in the boot of the car but dreaming is forever. And even if I swear, I swear I'll never be friends with an animal ever again dreaming is still forever and every day is okay but at night my friend comes out from wherever he hides all day and into my head and eats Little Georgia and Dad and Mamma one by one by one every night.

**An Open Letter of Apology
to Little Georgia: Volume One**

To my darling Little Georgia,

As you know I am now an adult.

Now that I am twenty-one and you are fifteen, I feel it is time for me to take a moment's respite from my important life to reflect upon our scars.

You are very pretty. Petite. Fine legs. Pert bosom. Big red smile. Probably should have had braces, but what matter that, unless you open your mouth? An action hardly necessary for the PDHPE lessons you so adore. And then of course, there's your scar.

I was six years old when you arrived from somewhere like an angry, wrinkly red currant. Sometimes I used to dress you in my doll's clothes. When you got too big I

119

would dress the cat in my doll's clothes. You may remember that you hated it equally.

Whilst *I* have long since put away childish things, on this day of reflection, I am reminded of our little spats over Polly Pockets. You would look at me with that glint in your big baby eyes and unleash your birth-order ambivalence. Stage One: you start hitting yourself and slapping your own face and scratching your arms with your tiny perfect nails until you are vermilion. Stage Two: eyes locked with mine you restage the Charge of the Light Brigade in our playroom, strewing it with *my* My Little Ponies (that I had won through the meritocracy of the *Sunday Telegraph* colouring-in competition). And screaming like you were dying. And smiling.

In Mamma would run. 'Aaahh! She's JUST a *BABY*!'

'No, please listen, you don't understand Mamma! Please!' My protests were as fruitless as poor Goody Proctor's. Mamma would scoop you up, and from the parapet of her shoulder you would stare at me, with the devil Abigail in your eyes and flip me the bird. And I knew you'd won. You always won.

Except one time I urinated in the bed when I was nine and told Mamma and Dad it was you.

I became embittered, utterly defenceless in the face of this assault on my integrity by you, baby Joseph McCarthy, with whom I shared my bedroom and my genes. My poor parents – may they rest in Annandale – bewitched by your dribbly chin and your unimaginably golden ringlets, your wobbly fat legs and your dimply bottom, were deaf to my pleas, to my logic and reason. No evidence, no graphs or deductive reasoning would drag my parents out of the lie-hole you had dug and buried them in.

So I did something. Something un-sisterly. It was, in a way, an experiment. A minor contribution to scientific enquiry. I had to know. Could you fly?

Cut to Yia Yia and Papou's house in Drummoyne, 1993. You are three and I am nine, but with the reading level of a twelve year old. Yia Yia and mother are downstairs in the kitchen, chain-smoking, eating *kourabiethes* and bitching about Papou. Upstairs, you and I are playing in Papou's room. It is not very stimulating.

'Look, a paperweight. This watch has a stretchy band. Papou your slippers smell like cheese.' Papou sits on a chair in the room with us, drinking Scotch whisky from little bottles he stole from the Ibis Hotel in Brisbane.

'I want to play on the bed,' you say.

I pick you up and place you in the sad indentation where Papou has slept alone for half a century. You take a moment to get your balance and then start bouncing. Bounce, bounce, bounce. I climb onto the bed, hold your little hands and we bounce together. Bounce, bounce, bounce, a little higher. You are smiling and you start to giggle, gaining confidence. I let go of your hands. Carpe diem.

I jump as high as I can, high into the air and plunge arse

first onto the single bed whose ancient springs exhale their second last breath under my weight and my truth.

You are facing me. As I land, the bed's springs spring for the last time, sending you heavenward. Your expression: betrayal. You fly high and backwards, through the open doorway at the end of the bed. Your tiny, precious body smashes into the wall outside the room, makes a mid-air right-hand turn and disappears. From the ensuing dull thud, I correctly infer that you have plummeted head first onto Papou's set of dead weights at the end of the hall.

I look at Papou. He looks at me. We know we have less than two seconds before our lives are changed forever. Panicked, we freeze. There is the tiniest, needle-eye, sliver of silence. And then it begins. Wailing. Your desperate, anguished wailing. Impossibly guttural and dog whistling at the same time.

I find a moment to calibrate the results of my experiment.

Hypothesis: Could you fly?

Results: Inconclusive.

Yia Yia and Mamma race up the stairs like cannon fire, screaming, fags erect. They look at you, bleeding all over the floor. Then at Papou and me. He, still frozen on the chair, I on the deathbed. Both of us now charged at a minimum with criminal negligence.

'WHAT THE FUCK HAPPENED?'

Papou and I have not discussed a strategy. Thankfully the bewildering rate at which you are losing blood from your head and turning the same colour as the ashen carpet diverts their attention from the suspects. Before I know what is happening we are all in the car on our way to The Children's Hospital.

I remember at this point that Yia Yia and Papou were about to leave for a wedding – before I tried to kill you that is. In the front seat of the car, Papou, driving solemnly, blood dripping off his best suit and mingling with his pungent aftershave, is Mafioso personified – only he is adamantly, violently and repeatedly admonished by Yia Yia from the back seat. Now, in the winter of his masculinity, Papou is too dithering for a life of crime. I am disappointed.

We get to The Children's Hospital, where we meet Father in the waiting room. We are ushered straight to the front of the queue, past a row of bedraggled children. Children with their fingers caught in tricycle spokes, children with bleary weepy eyes, children with extra arms and rashes and children with whooping cough, then, into a little room with likenesses of Bart and Lisa Simpson painted crudely on the walls. There kindly young paediatricians reconfigure your head with their new experimental skin glue. For all that blood, your battle scar is a mere but enduring centimetre.

It's all over in a flash. Yia Yia and Papou go, bloodied, to the end of the wedding and the world, and Mamma, Dad, you and I get in a taxi. Mamma, now partially sedated, finds a moment to mention how lucky we were to go straight to the front past all those poor other children. Father gently suggests that it might have something to do with Mamma's left tit, which has been dangling outside her dress and bra covered in coagulated baby's blood.

Georgia, I am sorry.

Sincerely,

Zoë

The Red Light

The Red Light

A little fly buzzed its way around the room. It bounced from wall to table to wall and then it flew up to the top of the cupboard and settled next to the flashing red light.

It nestled itself down next to the red light and it said to me, 'Zoë, see this red light? This red light is probably not a good thing.'

I had been left in the little room to read my script. I had just finished high school and was at my first audition. For reasons Mamma said no one would ever understand, I had been overlooked by NIDA so if I was ever going to be an actor I was going to have to make it on my own.

Of course all actors have to make sacrifices and take on jobs that aren't commensurate with their profound ability to move people. And I made my dollars working for a telecommunications company where my job was to dress in an extremely tight lycra onesie, which betrayed all the times I got drunk and ate kebabs and didn't go to the gym. The horrible thing was garnished with a giant skunk's head, that sat on my face and obscured ninety per cent of my vision. In this magnificent garb, I had to stand at St James station during peak hours, with my arm outstretched, attempting to hand out pamphlets and not be stampeded by the busy and in-no-way-sympathetic-to-my-situation commuters. It was good, honest work. And in some ways, I'd tell myself in my less depressed moments, it was a bit like acting. *Be* the lycra skunk. And I was sure as hell going to stop doing it the very second I got my first acting job.

And so there I was, at my first audition. Sitting by myself in a little room at a desk that was covered in cow-themed contact paper. A tiny window high above reminded me that outside it was summer and everyone else was probably swimming and having barbeques, and on top of the tall cupboard was a little plastic fan blowing little blue streamers towards me and this little black dome with a flashing red light.

Even though I had attended every drama lesson at school I couldn't remember what the teacher had said about what to do if you get overlooked for NIDA. So I went on a job-seeking website and searched for 'acting'. There was only one job.

Woman required for theatrical production. Rehearsals paid and catered. Must provide some elements of own costume.

Greg didn't even need to see my CV. He must have heard of my impressive Drama HSC mark.

An hour earlier I had left Annandale to head out to a farm. I hardly ever went any further than wherever we could get to in Mamma's car with the petrol sign flashing 'empty', but I really wanted to be an actor, so I printed out the directions Greg had sent me and I got on the train. As I sat on the train, I watched as all the houses and shops and factories slowly thinned out and became trees and bushes and streams.

I got off the train where Greg had told me to, and walked across a paddock. There was a big country house with a cobblestone footpath and stone arches at the front. But that wasn't where Greg lived. I walked past the farmhouse until I saw a little cottage. The outside of it looked like how Mamma shabby-chic-ed everything only not on purpose and it had a big rusting corrugated iron roof.

I knocked on the door.

'You must be Zoë,' said Greg, and I accepted his sweaty hand. He led me through the cottage, leaning on every doorframe and then pushing himself in the desired direction as though he had worked out the most energy efficient way to manoeuvre his unsettling form through the narrow, twisting building, like an obese astronaut wandering around his space station. As he did, his little purple shorts rode up in the middle, revealing what might have been the beginnings of a hairy testicle.

And now I was in the little room reading this script and trying to ignore the flashing red light, then trying to imagine everything *else* that that flashing red light on the little black dome could be, everything that wasn't a webcam. I couldn't think of a single thing so I tried to ignore it again.

Greg had decided to leave me alone to read the script. He'd left the room and closed the door. I didn't really seem to have a surplus of options, so I just sat there and read it.

Scene 7

Leanne was emotionally and physically scarred when she was younger. Some of those scars are on her face. As a result she now likes to hit people and call them names – especially Steve, her husband. Leanne is wearing thigh-high black patent leather fuck-me boots, fishnets ripped at the crotch and a leather corset. She's holding a whip. Her breasts are popping out of the corset so you can see her nipples.

Leanne cracks her whip on Steve who is cowering on the ground.

Leanne: Down Piggy, down!

Greg returns to the room with two cold cups of Milo. He

squeezes past me and sits on the other side of the desk. The desk was clearly designed for one person, leaving us awkwardly proximal.

He pushes a Milo in front of me.

'Thanks,' I say.

'What do you think?'

'It's very interesting. Did you write it?' I ask. I have no idea why I'm asking questions, only I figure if we're talking then that's way less scary than if we're not talking.

'Yeah. Do you think you can see yourself as a Leanne?'

'Maybe, it seems like a challenging role,' I say.

'Yeah, it's very challenging. Do you own any fuck-me boots? It's very important that Leanne has fuck-me boots.'

'To be honest, I'm not sure if I do.'

'That's okay,' said Greg, 'we can work something out.'

I can hear a clock ticking very loudly. It's reminding me how much more wrong it is when we're not talking, when we're just staring at each other across this tiny desk.

I pick up my Milo and take a big sip.

'Thanks for the Milo,' I say, 'I love Milo.' I don't, I hate it. I hate that the chocolate bits don't blend into the cold milk. It's just milk and a soggy crust of chocolate at the bottom.

'That's okay,' says Greg, smiling.

A pause. I can hear that damn clock again and I just stand up.

'Greg,' I say, 'Greg, I had no idea what the time was,

I have to go and see my Mum.'

'Really?'

'Yeah, she's sick.' What the hell am I saying? 'She's very sick in the hospital and I have to go and bring her an egg sandwich because she likes eggs and she won't eat the hospital food.'

Why so many lie details? I've completely stopped driving my mouth and my brain, there's a tiny sociopath behind the wheel now, a tiny sociopath having a panic attack.

Greg looks upset. Great. I've made him upset. Now I'm going to die.

'Wait here,' he says and closes the door as he leaves me alone in the tiny room.

How will he do it? He'll probably come back in and just strangle me from behind. Maybe with some sort of rope or possibly just with his bare pink hands. That's how I'll go. Lured into the trap of a sadistic pervert reading a script about Leanne and the last thing I'll ever say is a lie about Mamma being sick.

Greg comes back in the room. His clasped hands are hiding something.

Then he opens them. I look into his palm. He's holding an ornament. It is a bright orange nest tended by a little sparrow that seemed to have real feather stuck to it. And underneath the sparrow are five speckled pink eggs.

'Here,' he says, pressing it into my hands, 'give it to your mum.'

'To my mum?' I ask.

'Yeah, she likes eggs.'

I stare at him, and I burst into tears.

'Maybe you better go now. Go and see your mum.' Greg puts a very kind hand on my back and leads me back out of the little cottage.

I step into the bright summer light and I let it warm my face.

I'm not going to die and I just told a terrible lie about Mamma. Oh, and there's also the crippling guilt that has taken a stranglehold over my entire body for confusing a sexual torturer with a perfectly nice sexually curious lonely man.

'So, Zoë, I'd like to offer you the role, if you'll take it.'

I look at Greg. He might not be a rapist, but he certainly wasn't clear in his job ad.

'No, I don't think I do.' Greg's face dropped. He scratched his disappointed little head. Then he reached into his wallet and pulled out a fifty-dollar note.

'I understand. This is for your time today,' he said, handing me the cash.

Holy shit. My mind started spinning. Was I making a terrible mistake? Fifty dollars to just sit around terrified reading what was objectively quite a funny script even though it wasn't supposed to be.

'Is that what you'd pay for rehearsals?'

'No, it's seventy-five dollars per rehearsal, plus pizza.'

Could I do that? Could I come out to this farm once a week to humour a very sensitive if mildly disturbing man for seventy-five dollars?

'I'm sure you'll find someone who is just great,' I say as I wave goodbye.

On the train on the way home I start thinking of everything that little black dome with the red flashing light could have been. A small, personal gaming console I hadn't heard of. An up-market egg timer, security alarm, fancy computer mouse, some sort of medical device that surely Greg needed for something.

When I get home to Annandale, Mamma is waiting for me.

'How did it go?' she asks.

'It was pretty weird. The guy was a bit pervy, but turned out not in like a bad way, you know?'

Mamma was not impressed. Then she was even more not impressed as she pointed at the ornament in my hands. 'What is that?'

I laughed. 'It's actually for you. I told him you were sick in the hospital and he told me to give it to you.'

Mamma laughed.

'Was he trying to make me depressed? He is a sicko, trying to make someone in the hospital depressed with this terrible gift. Throw it away.'

I didn't look at it as I threw the little sparrow in the outside bin.

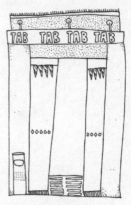

The Persistence of Memory

One chilly winter morning I woke up from the slumber of a twenty year old who has the world at her feet, but for some reason works at a discount menswear store. I pondered, unfondly, on the day that stretched out before me of selling cheaply made suits to men who probably shouldn't be proposing to their girlfriends.

After a little tiff with my sleepy, stubborn body, I managed to coax it out of bed. Just before I got to the kitchen to fix a breakfast of whatever the opposite of champions are, I caught a glimpse of myself in the mirror in the hallway.

How interesting, I thought, as I gazed upon my face. *The right side of my face looks normal, and the left side of my face looks like a basset hound.* I touched it, expecting it to be extremely tender, but it was rather more like poking a raw steak. A cold, dead steak.

I did a quick search of my brain to ascertain where this fit in the scheme of things my face should look like. I had on occasion awoken to realise that I had fallen asleep on a corduroy cushion, and then discovered, in the looking glass, a face blotted with deep and squiggly red lines. This was somewhat like that – if, following that event, someone had shot me in the left side of my face with a tranquiliser dart.

I walked to the kitchen and poured myself a bowl of cornflakes. I sat down to eat them and as I pushed a silvery spoon, quivering with milk and flakes, into my mouth, I thought: *How interesting.* Usually when I perform this rudimentary task, the cornflakes manage to remain in my mouth before embarking on a mysterious journey through my insides. They don't dribble slowly out onto the dining-room table making a very sad clumpy puddle of white and orange gunk. But my mouth couldn't close. Try as I might, the left side of my mouth just gaped slowly in and out, never fully opening or closing, like a fish out of water.

Georgia, who was fourteen at the time and had no understanding of what it meant to toil at a discount menswear store came into the room.

'Zoë...' she said as she gazed upon me and the mess I was still in the process of making on the floor. That's unusual, I thought as I watched her eyes widen in horror. My sister doesn't usually look at me like I'm dying.

'Zoë. Your face is broken.'

In comes Mamma. *Oh, Mamma*, I thought. She will bring a needed air of calmness and perhaps a fitting explanation for the circumstances. Mamma knows what's what.

That's weird. I thought, as Mamma took a step back from me, gasped, and burst into tears. Mamma doesn't usually behave like she's just watched ten puppies get stabbed when she comes to join me in a bowl of morning cornflakes. She ran out of the room and dialled the doctor. Then she marched me, still in my pyjamas, down the street to our local GP. I sat in the waiting room amongst a bunch of coughing old ladies and elderly men in grey woollen waistcoats who farted and read the various useless inserts from the paper that had been discarded by previous patients.

Occasionally one or another would look up at me, and their glances would linger on my face. *That's odd*, I thought. Usually it is I gazing upon these aged citizens of the community with a mixture of pity and dread, and it seems that the tables have turned.

Then my turn came. The doctor came out.

'Zoë?' she said, looking at me and then immediately down at her clipboard.

'Right this way.'

'It seems half of my face is broken,' I told the doctor, as

I sat down in the little white room, adorned with crayon pictures and photos of toddlers. She pulled out a packet of baby wipes and considered my face with a mild mixture of sorrow and disgust, like a pigeon that had been run over by a bicycle. Not quite dead, but certainly not quite right.

'I think you have Bell's Palsy.'

'What's that?'

'No one really knows.'

'Is there anything I can do?'

'Take steroids.'

'What will they do?'

'Look, probably nothing, but they will make you put on quite a lot of weight.'

'In that sense, those steroids are a bit like fifty Big Macs.'

'I suppose.'

'Is there anything else I should know?'

'You'll need to buy an eye patch.'

'Why?'

'Because your left eye will weep a constant stream of tears until it goes away.'

'When will it go away?'

'Who can say. Could be a month, could be seven years.'

I left the doctor's surgery with a prescription for steroids and another for heavy painkillers, which I definitely didn't need, but I dutifully took, because when science tells me I am allowed drugs, I am at her mercy.

At the chemist I also bought my eye patch, which I found out soon after, would be my best friend – if one's best friend made one look like a sad pirate.

As a twenty year old, I had been, until that very morning, skipping merrily down the same sexy path of experimentation as my friends. Then two roads diverged in a yellow wood. While my friends learned that men can be cruel, I learned that sometimes when you go into a shop people feel sorry for you and give you stuff for free. My friends were in Cancun and I was in a Kafka story.

I quickly learned the following about Bell's Palsy: It makes half your face look like Salvador Dali's melting clocks. Doctors really don't know anything about it, but they'll chemically fatten you while you have it because there's a character building exercise somewhere in the Hippocratic Oath. Tissues are your constant bedfellow due to the Bell's Palsy mouth maxim: What goes in, must dribble slowly out.

I tried my best to maintain a normal, *Sex and the City* inspired social life. On Friday night I'd go out for drinks with my girlfriends. Camilla would tell us how the Chilean bartender downstairs just asked for her number and I'd tell the gang about Mamma crying while watching me try to drink through a straw.

Of all the people in my life, myself included, Mamma was the most upset by my new face. She even took it upon herself to do some internet research. She had discovered a PDF created by a university in Europe with some helpful advice on how to rehabilitate people with Bell's Palsy. It included things like forcing them to chew with the affected side of their mouth, trying to whistle and, of course, trying to drink through a straw. If I had bothered to look it up myself, I'm reasonably confident that I would have discovered that the PDF had in fact been created by the mean older brother of someone with Bell's Palsy, for all those tasks were in equal measure demeaning and impossible.

Formerly, at the discount menswear store, I had struggled to move the acres of polyester t-shirts emblazoned with wilfully awful slogans like 'One Tequila, Two Tequila, Three Tequila, Floor', but my new face, which was essentially half a wheel of brie that had been left in the sun and dressed up as a pirate, seemed to evoke a level of pity which induced people to give us money. My canny manager recognised my newfound salesmanship and paraded me around the store like a curious street beggar. She even took me off probation, which meant upgrading my uniform from a polo shirt that said 'Trish' on the pocket to one that said 'Zoë' on the pocket.

My new shirt filled me with pride, and philosophy. I began to become surprisingly self-reflective and ponderous for a sexually excitable twenty-year-old girl.

So, Bell's Palsy. It was going to be my thing. It wasn't great, but it could have been worse. I could have been one of those people with an annoying affectation, like always carrying around a ukelele. It probably didn't bode well for my already fruitless attempts to acquire a mate through the tried and tested method of never making eye contact with a man. Cheerfully, things were so barren in that department that this turn of events surely couldn't make things worse. Perhaps I could even garner a sympathy vote from a biology student, I thought, hopefully.

I even briefly attempted a gym regimen. Each workout would leave a deep and lasting purple legacy all over my face for at least two hours. Also, each session seemed to bring my breasts one inch closer to my knees, and I already had enough problems in the arena of sagging, so I swapped it for drinking myself into a blissful oblivion.

The days and the months passed and leaves turned from green to brown to rot just like the left side of my face, and I grew fatter in dribbling self-acceptance. My friends got used to my expanding form and constantly having to pass me napkins to wipe away the litres of Long Island Ice Tea dribbling down my shirt. I even managed on one occasion to lure a drunk man, who probably had a thing for pirates, back to my spider web.

And one day, in this state of inner peace I walked into a Gloria Jean's to buy a coffee.

'NOOOOOOOOOOOOOOOO!!!' A man screamed as I approached the counter.

I was used to pity but never before had my face provoked a response of unbridled terror in a fully-grown adult. And

I shot him the most severe dirty look I was capable of.

I went to leave, and then time froze. I couldn't move. My feet were melding into the floor. Either I was having a night terror or Bell's Palsy had migrated to my feet.

I did an inventory of my surroundings. The lights were off. There were no pastries in the darkened counter. I looked back to the entrance and I could see my own footprints. Was I going mad?

I started to feel sick. Like my lungs were filling with chemicals. Which they definitely were.

'What have you done?!' screamed the screaming man with the singular devastation of someone who had, mere moments before, finished several days' work varnishing the floor of a brand new Gloria Jean's, and now watched helplessly as someone walked in and completely ruined it in an instant.

I looked at him he looked at me. I started to try to run, but very slowly like the sticky Pompeii victim I had become and gradually progressed away from the screaming man who save from a fist shaking in the air, dared not move, lest he make things worse.

I got outside and tried to walk away, casually, although my sticky footprints leading directly back to the scene of the crime made travelling incognito a challenge. So I called Mamma, who drove over and picked me up a short and sticky distance away from the incident.

We were stopped in the car at a set of lights. Mamma

looked at me and started crying. Great. This is just what I need for my inner peace.

'Your mouth!' she said.

'I know.'

'No. It looks a little bit more normal!'

I looked in the passenger mirror. It wasn't exactly a *TV Week* smile, but there might have been some movement at the station. I looked at Mamma again.

'You think it's better?'

She considered me for a moment and then started crying again.

'I'm so sorry. I made a mistake. It's still the same.'

'Well...Damn,' I said.

I wound down the window and put my face to the wind and I just let it flap about however it wanted to.

The Devil Wears a
Denim Winter One-Piece

After decades of corruption, bad bookkeeping, fraud and grievous mistreatment of staff, the Children's Drama Company finally became insolvent and died. But not before I had a chance to work there when it was in the throes of its last attempt to wreak unhappiness and alcoholism on the world.

It was a great job on paper. I was the Head Creative. I had no idea what that meant, largely because it didn't mean a thing, but it would make for excellent business cards. My friend Chris had handed the job down to me. On my first day he helped me clean the skin, fingernails and red wine off my inherited keyboard, which was connected to a hulking grey cube that whirred loudly as if to say 'I swear, I am a computer.' Chris helped me tear down some rotting brown curtains, and showed me where the filing cabinets were. Then he fucked off to the Isle of Wight.

He left me with LaReine.

Before I started my job I'd heard two things on the grape vine about LaReine. The first was that neither she nor the company paid taxes. The second was that one time she'd invited herself over to the house of a prominent art gallery curator where she'd tried to teach herself how to make martinis then shat on his new white couch, after which she locked herself in his bathroom until he had to call the police to have her removed. I had no idea if either of those things was true, but they made me very excited for my first day of work.

LaReine was born into an old aristocratic family from Richmond Upon Thames and, from what I understood, was basically a Tudor. Some people said she'd been exiled to Australia to start the company, to save the reputation of a famous actor she'd somehow convinced to sleep with her. LaReine was a slender, ageless giantess. It wasn't so much that she looked young but that she was such a strange and singular human being that made it very hard to take a stab at her vintage. Did LaReine grow up watching *Coronation Street*? Did she remember the invention of the fax machine? The Battle of the Somme? I couldn't say.

LaReine had a costume that she wore every day. It was

a denim winter one-piece accessorised with four pairs of glasses, one on her face and three in the furious mass of steel wool that was her hair.

When I first started, I was LaReine's only employee. We each had our own office in a building that was leased cheaply to artists, where she had somehow wrested two rooms away from actual artists. On my first day LaReine walked into my office, raised her leg from the confines of her denim winter one-piece and kicked my handbag across the room. Then she looked up at me and said, 'I shouldn't have done that…That was rude.'

That was the only communication we had all day.

For the first few weeks I thought her central problem was that she was insane. I once asked her for the pin code to the photocopier. She wrote down on a piece of paper '567832' while saying '145390'. Her computer was never on, but it was always covered in post-it notes. I tried to explain to her that there was actually a program inside the computer that made digital post-it notes. This seemed to make her angry and taught me that initiative was not what she was looking for in her employee. She ran into my office one morning and accused me of taking her glasses. I asked if she possibly meant the ones on her eyes or the three in her hair. She didn't understand but left me alone for the rest of the day.

As weird as things had started out, they took a nose dive when we lost a huge grant. Despite our claims, the grant body had no reason to believe we were really a charity. This was partly because we didn't have legal charity status and partly because we didn't do anything charitable. I sat in the meeting pretending to take notes while LaReine cried and said things like, 'I am a charity!!?' and 'How could it be lawful for you not to give me money?' and 'Well, you better know, you've made me really mad. I'm really mad now.' None of this seemed to help.

After we lost the grant LaReine started sending me emails like: 'If you're [sic] pay hasn't gone in, it's because it was really windy today and that effects [sic] the internet.' I bumped into her once at a pub. I said hi, and she stared at me, blankly, with absolutely no idea who I was. Even though I'd said goodbye to her only fifteen minutes earlier, and even though we were each other's only colleagues.

'LaReine, it's Zoë. From work?'

'Oh…These aren't all for me,' she said, pointing to five bottles of wine on the take-away counter.

'Look, the whole gang is here.' She said attempting to divert my attention by waving to some people at the bar that neither of us knew.

The true extent of her evilness only became apparent when we started working with other people. We ran ludicrously expensive week-long drama programs for students, and at the end of each day, she'd convince the volunteer tutors to stay back for a drink. She'd charge them five dollars per glass for wine that was not only donated to the company, but also corked. When one tutor got sick of it and brought in his own wine, she took it out of his bag and sold it to the other tutors.

Being the mediator between LaReine and hundreds of students, parents, drama teachers and volunteer staff, was a diplomatic nightmare. I once spent half an hour on the phone trying to console a mother, who had received something close to a death threat from LaReine because the woman's son was a vegetarian. LaReine evidently thought this would send the workshop lunch breaks into unmitigated chaos and when she calmed down enough to plan, she told me to remove the slice of of slimy packet ham from one of the ham and cheese sandwiches.

LaReine only once displayed something that I think was meant to be compassion. It was in an email she sent me regarding the recent employment of a staff member which included the memorable lines, 'Fire her after Christmas. Christmas time is hard for her, abusive father et cetera et cetera.'

By the time of the National Drama for Youth Festival, I had managed to convince LaReine to hire my best friend Camilla. To bring a normal-functioning human being into the company, was a markedly cruel thing to do on my part, but as it had been a chum who had gotten me into this hideous circumstance, I thought it was only fair to pay this shit sandwich forward. And selfishly, I was thrilled to finally have someone on the inside.

I don't know much about child protection laws but I can tell you that many things happened at the National Drama for Youth Festival, and I'd be incredibly surprised if any of them were legal. The centrepiece of the festival involved bringing about fifty school kids from all over regional Australia to the middle of Sydney, ditching them in a hotel for two weeks, in an area closely associated with raging clubs, gang violence and heroin, and telling them they definitely couldn't drink.

Making sure this didn't happen was my responsibility. I've deliberately repressed the details of this festival, so all I can tell you are the facts on public record. I made six trips to St Vincent's hospital, and lost more than one kid on a train.

Back at the office, Camilla's relationship with LaReine had rapidly deteriorated after her $2000 cheque for building the company's website had 'blown away in the wind'. Camilla began an investigation. She pored through the company's filing cabinets and discovered that we were being sued for $30,000 in unpaid superannuation. It was hard to piece the whole story together from the maniacal clippings in the filing cabinet, but Camilla reckoned that as far as she could tell, the company used to be funded by a wealthy playboy who disappeared in the Bahamas in 1994. She also told me, with no small measure of fear, that she couldn't find any record of where LaReine was during that particular year.

It was around the night that Camilla and I were crying outside LaReine's office, rubbing peanut butter on her door handle and drinking a bottle of donated wine that we decided things had to change. We were becoming LaReine. We called in a member of the company's largely inactive board for a mediation session. We thought that if they could only see how evil LaReine was they might see fit to end her regime. In the middle of the session LaReine looked straight at Camilla and said: 'I, I, I, I...HATE you!' We looked pleadingly at the board member for some sign that she comprehended what had just happened, but she kept taking notes.

Camilla and I continued on after the unsuccessful mediation session, plotting to kill LaReine. Our hairdresser Tracey gave us a recipe to make a tea using daddy-long-legs that she claimed would serve as an undetectable poison. Once after a meeting with LaReine, which she'd insisted on having at the pub and where she told us we were both getting a pay cut, I really did almost kill her. As LaReine turned to leave down a flight of stairs, Camilla planted her hands firmly on mine when she realised I was perilously close to pushing her down.

'We don't need any witnesses,' she said.

The final straw came when LaReine skipped town and left us to organise another festival without money, staff or contact information for the two-hundred students and teachers. After pulling in favours from every living friend, family member and bus driver we knew, something happened which almost looked like a festival.

When LaReine returned, a meeting was called to debrief. It coincided with a funeral Camilla and I had to go to. I sent LaReine an email explaining the situation and she wrote back one line:

'The meeting is at 6pm. All funerals are over by 6pm.'

Ten minutes later she sent a follow-up email that said:

'Also I am sorry for your loss.'

After that half my face collapsed. Again. Having previously had Bell's Palsy, which I was assured could not occur twice, a neurology report determined that I didn't have a brain tumour, the only other option. There was no medical explanation for my condition. LaReine had made my face collapse.

Camilla and I quit after that and three months later the company filed for bankruptcy.

Two years on I bumped into LaReine on the street. In an unfortunate and unprecedented moment of clarity she seemed to recognise me. She looked at me and said, 'My mum just ran over my dad,' and turned around and walked off into the setting sun.

The Alive Pile

So there I am one day, in a particularly depressing shopping centre. It has a swathe of clothing stores nobody has heard of and too many two-dollar shops. It's waiting patiently, with its stale spring-roll providores and ghastly costume jewellery stores, for Westfield to come and put it out of its misery. But I'm nineteen and I make my way teaching a handful of kids how to play the French horn and trumpet to a middling standard and for not very much money so I can't really afford so shop anywhere else. I'm there, at the sad shopping centre, about to get a garish manicure from a fifteen year old. But before I do I go to the bathroom. I've just drunk about a litre of warm, flat no-name lemonade and now I'm doing a giant wee and contemplating what ungodly hue I'm about to inflict on my nails…And then it begins.

'Help me! Please help me!'

A damsel in distress? My mind begins to race. A drug deal gone awry? A woman going into labour? Whatever which way, some lady needs me.

'Are you okay? With you in a sec.'

'No! NOW! I need help NOW!'

'I'm mid wee…'

'AAAHHHHH!'

I've never been able to stop mid wee before or since, but there was something in this stranger's scream that made time and wee stand still. I busted into the next cubicle, and there she was. A tiny old woman, whom I would later come to know as Lilith – partly because she was evil, and partly because that was her name – had fallen arse first into the toilet. Her skinny little legs and slippers flailing out in front at me, her arms clutching the cistern, her body all but submerged in the bowl.

I reach over and grab her under the arms and begin to pull. She claws at my face, like a cat. Once she's out she tells me her name and pulls fifty dollars out of the pocket in her red-chequered pinafore. She holds the fifty out at me in her bony, shaking hand. Aside from the shaking and the general ravages of age, with her tiny stature and her hair in two little buns, Lilith looks like a six year-old girl.

'Is this enough to get some bananas?'

'Sure. How many?'

'Bananas.'

'Yeah, how many bananas?'

'Is this enough for bananas?'

'Yes, absolutely, as long as you don't need, you know, sixty of them.'

'Bananas.'

So Lilith is a bit mad. This is a shame. I have several trumpet students coming to my house this afternoon and Lilith is looking up at me, piss all over her dress, scrunching a fifty-dollar note in my face.

'My name is Lilith.'

'That's great. Where do you live?'

'Bananas?'

I am at a crossroads. I can help Lilith find her way home, lose my students and compromise their already precarious trust – I am not a very good or reliable trumpet teacher. In fact, strictly speaking, I don't play the trumpet, I play the French horn, and not very well. Or I can leave her sodden and disoriented, thrusting money at people who may not be as altruistic as me, in this mirthless shopping centre. While I've been thinking I realise that Lilith is on the move. I hear 'Bananas?' coming from the men's bathroom. I've never pulled anyone out of the toilet before, except for Georgia, so I feel a certain responsibility setting in. I burst into the men's.

161

'She's with me.'

A man in his forties shakes his dribbling willy at me like a stern finger, in a way that can only mean, 'That's no way to take care of your grandmother.'

Lilith is clutching his arm.

'Come on Lilith,' I say. She looks at me and then at the man. She brushes her hand over his arm, staring at his dick. She is flirting with him. Eventually I get her out of there. We're walking toward the exit, past Dresses by Dorothy and Sandals World. She is so slow I could punch her in the face, make a cup of tea and catch her before she hit the ground. Then she stops halfway to the exit and bursts into tears.

'Lilith, what's wrong?'

'My stick! My stick!'

'It's okay Lilith, it's probably still in the bathroom, I'll get it for you.'

She stops crying. 'Go on then,' she says.

I'm starting to realise that yes, Lilith may be crazy, but she's also cunning and a brat. I retrace my steps and sure enough there somehow in the toilet bowl, all foamy with pee, is Lilith's stick, standing there like the saddest flagpole in the world. I grab it, shake it, and take it back to her.

'My name is Lilith,' she says grabbing the stick. She starts limping heavily on her right side. She has had no trouble walking until now. At the foot of the stairs, near the exit, she bursts into tears.

'Stairs! Stairs!' She howls and clutches my shirt. I look back. People are staring at me and the streaky line of piss-water dripping off her pinafore and stick that marks our long and boring journey across the floor. With a great deal of unease I half carry, half push her up the stairs. When we're outside I hail a cab, which again I have to assist her into. I knead her body into the back seat. She looks up at me with puppy-dog eyes, and points to her legs which are dangling out of the cab.

My patience is wearing. I lift up her stupid legs, do up her seatbelt and climb in the front.

The driver looks at me, furious. I realise the stench of urine has already filled his cab. I also realise that I have no plan.

'Listen, I'm just trying to help this woman get home.'

'Bananas.'

'Can we drive down the main road? I need to get her some bananas and then work out where she lives and take her home.'

'We don't stop for bananas,' says the driver.

'Listen mate, I'm trying to do the right thing here.

'No bananas.'

'Bananas!'

'Jesus, I'll leave my bag in the car, I promise I'll be back.'

'Listen lady, this is a cab. Not a bananas. No bananas.'

'I'll give you twenty bucks.'

I'll insert a banana into your penis, you greedy bad Samaritan, I think to myself, as he agrees to my terms.

We drive, I stop in at a fruit shop for bananas and then the cab ambles aimlessly down the road.

'STOP! STOP!' cries Lilith.

'Is this where you live?'

'Yes!'

She runs out of the cab. I pay the driver and follow her in. Today I'm not wearing my glasses, and by the time I walk into what eventually reveals itself to be a podiatry clinic, Lilith is running up the stairs like fucking Usain Bolt. The kindly receptionist suggests she might live at the Christian mission down the street and after some coaxing I get her out of the clinic. As we walk down to what I pray is where she lives, she remembers her chronic walking ailments and we resume our right-biased snail pace.

Eventually I start to see old people spilling out onto the streets in pyjamas and sometimes no pants. There is a man sitting on the bench outside the mission in an open robe, tugging at his ancient, tiny penis and crying quietly – I'm at Lilith's place and it's pretty much the saddest thing I have ever seen.

'Lilith!' the man splutters through his tears.

'Hi Bill.' She starts like she's about to leave and then hesitates.

'Don't tell anyone about this!' she says desperately.

'Sure…' I say, and as she runs inside, I go in search of a staff member.

Inside, the building is painted a sickly yellow and the walls are postered with various messages, in big, bold print, all hygiene related. It smells like very strong disinfectant has intermingled with every kind of corporal secretion but failed to make any of them disappear. I eventually find someone whose eyes move together as a pair and whose privates are completely covered in clothes that have clearly been bought from a shop.

Her name is Miss Lucy. Miss Lucy is tall and comforting in her white muslin dress and I stand with her in the stinkng, yellow foyer and tattle on Lilith. She looks at me warmly.

'You're such a good person, come upstairs and Miss Lucy will make you some tea.' It turns out Miss Lucy always refers to herself in the third person, which makes her seem like a teacher and inspires in me a need to please her.

My students must have given up on me by now. I briefly consider what it will be like to be fired by a string of nine year olds, but I am mesmerised by Miss Lucy's muslin-wrapped buttocks and I follow up the stairs in a trance.

'Good people like you are a gift to this world,' she says, pouring me a cup of tea. 'Drink your tea. Such a gift. So much pretty hair. '

Before I know it I have signed a piece of paper committing me to giving my free time to the place on a regular basis. As I walk out of there past all the semi-clothed inhabitants I'm feeling many things that sit uneasily with one another. I'm smug about becoming a Charitable Person, I'm slightly annoyed that I've been grossly manipulated by Miss Lucy and I'm terrified about coming back and seeing Lilith again, who I'm sure will hate me when she realises I have betrayed her.

Nevertheless, over the next few weeks I volunteer my time to this place and its people. On my first day, I arrive ready to read Elizabeth Gaskell and cut the crusts off sandwiches. Miss Lucy meets me in the foyer.

'First thing Zoë, you must give everyone a basic dental check up.'

'Miss Lucy, what could you possibly mean?'

'Oh you know, just assess the state of their dental health and make some notes.'

'You know, strictly speaking Miss Lucy, I am not a dentist.'

'Miss Lucy has faith in you.'

Miss Lucy left, and I went around to anyone who looked more like they lived there than worked there.

'When was the last time you saw a dentist?'

'Never.'

'How long has that slimy bulging black thing been where all your bottom teeth should be?'

'I love you.'

'Hello there, I—'

'Don't touch me.'

'How long has your mouth been bleeding like that?'

'Nobody is my friend.'

'Do you have a tooth brush?'

'Yeah, and I'm going to brush your hair with it.'

'Now can you just open your mouth and show me your teeth?'

Through waves of nausea, I let twenty old people who have never seen a dentist breathe all over me. My clothes smell like rotting dog food dripping with saliva as I make feeble notes on my clipboard about how many more seeping mouth ulcers they all have than teeth.

My mission work continues over the next few weeks. Sometimes I sit at the front counter and give the more threatening residents my money. Sometimes I check the dinner plates for false teeth.

On what would be my last day at the mission Miss Lucy says, 'Zoë, today you're going to separate these photos of the residents into two piles. Those who are alive and those who are dead. Then laminate the ones who are alive and shred the ones who are dead. Here is a paper shredder.'

A photo of Judith, she looks so happy with her big gummy smile and watermelon earrings. Into the shredder. A photo of Jim sitting on a park bench with a pigeon. See ya Jim. A photo of Joselyn dressed up like a vampire for Halloween. Gone. After a while I begin to imagine that maybe I am Death. If I shred the wrong photo, will Bill set his pyjamas on fire and drink a bottle of Pine-O-Clean?

Then I see a photo of Lilith. She hasn't spoken to me since
I started working there. Because of me she lost all her privi-
leges and can't go outside anymore. When I tried to check
her teeth she threw a snakes-and-ladders board at me. In the
photo she is wearing a floral dress and matching hat. She
snarls at me like a nasty reedy snake that has just eaten a
dog. I take her over to the shredder. I stare into her wrinkly
ungrateful eyes and hold her over my death machine. And
then I think better of it. I laminate her stupid face and
reluctantly put her in the 'Alive' pile.

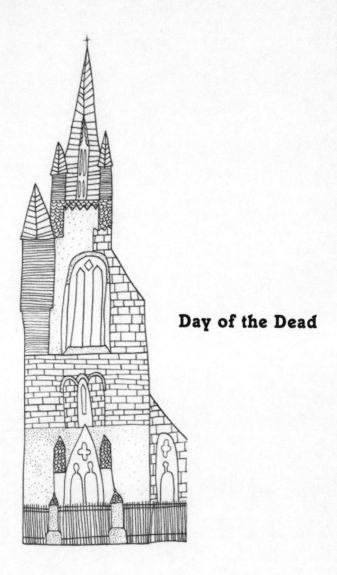

Day of the Dead

Watching someone grieve can be a terrifying and enlightening thing. The news arrives like a bag of shit exploding in slow motion on your face. Then tremendous shock, and then clarification is called for again and again. Then everything is viscera, viscera and mucus and somebody puts the kettle on, then more people arrive. And at some point a joke is made, a little joke or an anecdote is told by someone, a joke that causes the griever to crack a smile briefly, maybe even laugh as everything is temporarily forgotten, and then it returns, amplified as if it is being heard again for the first time. That's why bereavement counsellors are so important, and why it is such a shame that my relatives think it's appropriate to leave messages that people have died on the answering machine.

When I was twelve I found this message on our answering machine:

'Hi Koula, I mean Thea, I mean Donna. It's Papou. Niko is dead. See you soon!'

Out in the kitchen Mamma was stirring.

'Mamma...When's dinner?'

'About five minutes Zoë.'

'Cool. Who's Niko?'

'You know Niko darling, he's my lovely God-brother. You know him, he's a brilliant athlete.'

'Nope. Cool, anyway he's dead.'

Mamma stared at me dumbfounded. Tears in her eyes. And as she retreated to her room to cry on the bed, I thought to myself: that spaghetti is going to burn and stick to the pot and there'll be no dinner for anyone. Did I possess the savoir-faire to open a packet of cheese and put it on a plate in light of Mamma's compromised ability to parent effectively? As I look back now at my sad and 'big-boned' twelve-year-old self, desperately eating bits of sweaty cheese and plastic wrapping, I now understand that memory as the hideous prophecy that it was.

On the day of the funeral, Mamma laid out one of her dresses on my bed for me to wear. It was like two dresses, one tight and satiny, the other sheer and spider-webby. I borrowed her red lipstick and a pair of thick ugly heels.

Then, all dressed up, like a mid-range prostitute, and with no concept of who the fuck Niko was or whether I'd ever met him, we got in the car and started to drive. Almost immediately I had a horrible feeling in my gut. Something wasn't right. Mamma had forgotten to make breakfast. And so bewildered and hungry, Mamma drove us to the Greek Parish and Community of St Spyridon in Kingsford.

In the church, mourners lined up to kiss a picture of Mary. I looked at Mamma, who had sheltered me from all things religious, for a one-off piece of spiritual guidance.

'Just go up to the picture, kiss it and cross yourself.'

I did. Then came the scowling and pointing. I looked at Mamma who was drawing her thumb across her throat in homicidal discouragement.

'Your right hand!' she whispered emphatically and all too late, as if I was supposed to know instinctively that crossing myself with my left hand was tantamount to putting a kitten dressed up as Jesus in the microwave. I looked away from the snarling Yia Yias judging me with their loud Greek injunctions.

The church was filled with hundreds of people who had come to say goodbye to the mysterious Niko. We were directed to the front pews, because apparently we were very close family. Even his giant portrait propped against the coffin didn't trigger any memories. Deciding it wasn't the time or the place to nudge my neighbour and say 'Hey, how do we know this guy again?' I just sat down and tried to blend in. There were two robed priests standing on either side of the coffin. One spoke in regular Greek, the other in what I assume was old-timey Greek, but could have been Latin or incredibly broken English for all I knew. This was our guy, and every time he spoke, he swung a smoking can of something religious-smelling back and forth, while incanting:

Sto onomou tou Patrou.

Tou Dieu.

Kai Agio Nevmata.

At mysterious intervals everyone would stand up and sit down, and stand up and sit down. As I tried to copy them, I thought about that can. I wasn't sure what was supposed to be in it. Maybe God's breath? But it smelled kind of familiar, like the way our toilet smells after Mamma's cleaned it. And a bit like the way the hospital smelled when Yia Yia had some of her bowel removed. The more I thought about it I realised that maybe this guy had run out of God's breath, and if he had, what would he do? He couldn't very well go up to the close relative of mine who organised Niko's funeral and say, 'Hey listen I'm shit out of God's breath.' No, he'd probably go straight to the holy cleaning cupboard, find the mop bucket and fill his can up and then set it on fire somehow.

Sto onomo tou Patrou.

Yeah I'm onto you, buddy, I thought. I stared at the impostor, angry, hungry and nauseous. Then I realised I had confused feelings of anger with the impending certainty that I was going to pass out. And vomit. I could only hope that I passed out first. Which I did. Right on the four feet and eleven inches of Mamma. In an act of equal parts humiliation and tremendous physical strength, she dragged me down the aisle of the church as I gurgled out vomit.

I regained consciousness again just in time for the end of the service. I skirted around my vomit and joined the line of close family, to stand, be kissed and consoled by the mass of mourners.

'I'm so sorry for your loss,' strangers whispered to me as they kissed me on both cheeks.

'This will be a very difficult time for you but you have to stay strong,' said a nice old man.

'Thank you,' I said with my best sad voice.

We drove to the graveyard to bury the coffin. Ominous storm clouds emerged from nowhere cloaking the sky in a big Greek mourning gown. By the time the coffin was lowered, it was pouring. People threw dirt on Niko's coffin. I picked up a handful – with my right hand – and hurled it with attempted solemnity. A strong wind coming from the other direction cast clumps of it back into my face. On the plus side, it was harder to see the vomit once I was in blackface.

By the time I got to the wake I'd basically done the eight-hour famine. In the dining room I spotted my Yia Yia in a blue rinse of old ladies and snacks. I sat down next to her and feverishly ate a big plate of bread and red sauce. Yia Yia glared at me. So what if I'd eaten a whole plate of bread and delicious red sauce? I know wogs. There was more bread. There was always more bread.

'What? No one else wants any.'

'Zoë,' said Yia Yia, 'that was the body of Christ. You just ate the body of Christ. The whole body of Christ.'

Nobody would make eye contact with me, except Yia Yia whose mouth was pinched and her eyes steely. And Jesus went, uncomplaining, down my oesophagus.

Mamma came in.

'She ate Jesus.'

Mamma looked at Yia Yia. Then at me as she sighed and wiped some of Jesus' blood off my face. She bought me a KFC Fun Bucket on the way home.

It was not long after that that Dad's mother, Nanna Mildred, finally died. I knew it had happened because I found this message from Uncle Bryn on our answering machine:

'A bit of bad news…see, well, Mam's dead.'

And with the sensitivity of a brick shattering a window, I walked into the lounge room, looked at Dad, reposed on the settee, half asleep watching *Friends* and said to the back of his head that his Mam was dead. That I didn't know when or how. But his brother had left a message.

Nanna Mildred had almost died quite a number of times before she finally committed to the plan. This was a logistical nightmare, because she lived in Wales and we lived in Annandale. Each time she threatened to go through with it, Dad would pack a carry-on suitcase and make his way from Annandale to the little Council flat on the other side of the world. And each time, with just a little coaxing, she would claw her way back from her certain death, and Dad would come home. Until the time I got the message on the answering machine.

By her own reports, Mamma had a pretty lousy experience when she went over to meet Nanna Mildred for the first time in 1978. At that point, Nanna had gone a bit spare. She quickly became convinced that Mamma was a gypsy and that she was stealing her silverware. She had mistaken gypsy for Greek and silverware for a few lard encrusted sporks. And she had mistaken stealing for washing. They stayed in the suffocating little flat together for about a fortnight, and every night Dad would abandon the two women downstairs where they would watch *Dallas* and hate each other. He occupied his evenings secretly whittling a massive hole in a giant cube of soap with the intention of stuffing it with hash and smuggling it into France. Nanna Mildred and Mamma only really had one thing in common. Chain smoking.

Dad had moved to Australia in the seventies, leaving his brother Bryn to deal with Nanna Mildred, or as they called her, Mam.

Every Sunday Bryn would let himself in and sit down

in Mam's chair, its arms pocked with hundreds of cigarette burns. He'd pull out his little machine and get to work rolling enough cigarettes to get Mam through to the next Sunday. She had rheumatoid arthritis and refused to smoke tailor-mades. Mam would be in the kitchen peeling potatoes and her fingers into a pot bubbling with beef, peas and lard. She was close to legally blind but had the hearing of an Alsatian.

Uncle Bryn liked rolling cigarettes. It made it easier to avoid conversation. She'd serve up two modest plates of glistening meat bits and greeny-white mush. They'd sit down in silence for a few bites.

'Did you record my programs?' she would ask, accusingly.

'Of course Mam.' The woman had her own means of circumventing communication. Bryn would pop in a tape of *Home and Away* and they'd continue eating.

'Don Fisher is a bastard.'

'No doubt Mam.'

'That Pippa is a good woman. Imagine that. Five foster children.'

'God be with them, Mam.'

And so was Bryn's lot.

The last time Nanna Mildred almost died, Dad packed his little wheelie bag and made the adventure from Kingsford Smith to Cardiff Central Station. By this point the woman was a veritable medical exhibition, riddled with everything imaginable, to the point of being almost more ailment than lady. Dad travelled with every confidence that this would be the last time. Nanna Mildred was snuggled up sickly in Barry Hospital, a place where wee and golden staph seemed to ooze out of the walls, Uncle Bryn explained when he picked Dad up from the station. He also issued Dad with a troubling warning.

'The thing is Paul. Well, Mam stinks. You see, Mam stinks quite bad.'

Nanna Mildred had a lot of problems at this point. They ranged roughly from itchy to terminal in nature and included, somewhere along the list, flatulence of the most noxious and noisome order. She was now legally blind and had taken to wearing a sweaty yellowing wig. Dad used to be the Infected Rubbish Man at a hospital when he was in his twenties, which basically involved being in charge of disposing of bits of people that had been lanced or chopped off. He wasn't sure how he would deal with the revolting wig, but Dad was confident that he was medically experienced enough to stoically endure the farting.

Dad was wrong. The ferocity of Nanna Mildred's farts was in fact, more than Dad and all other surveyed humans could bear, and so he and Bryn hatched a little plan. After Dad had spent about an hour with Nanna, reacquainting himself after the year or two that had passed, he and Bryn excused themselves and went on a trip to the local shop, where they bought several bottles of air freshener in varying floral notes.

Over the next few weeks, the air freshener went part of the way to masking the magnificent and ever changing smells emanating from Nanna Mildred's bottom. Her blindness had of course made the spraying of air freshener over well-timed coughing fits possible without her noticing, but it also had a curious by-product that no-one was expecting.

'Who has been bringing me flowers?' she asked, one day.

The room, of course, was completely absent of flowers, or cards, for no-one really liked Nanna Mildred.

'Ah, the postman, Ma,' said Bryn, quickly.

'I hate the postman,' said Nanna Mildred, before smiling to herself and falling asleep.

Each day, Dad and Bryn would have to invent new suitors who had supposedly brought Nanna flowers while spraying the room.

'I hate roses. I hate Richard Jones. I hate cousin Alfred. I hate the Welsh Rugby Team,' Nanna Mildred would say, day after day, while inhaling air freshener, before closing her eyes and dipping her toes into whatever fantasy my father and Uncle Bryn had cultivated for her that day.

A few weeks later, Nanna Mildred had seemingly gotten all the farts out of her system. So she put on her housecoat and toddled back home to continue amongst the living. And by living, I mean *Home and Away's* Alf and Pippa, tinned kippers, hand-rolled cigarettes and Uncle Bryn. Satisfied that Nanna Mildred seemed to be more alive than dead, Dad bid them farewell and went home to Annandale.

If you didn't know them, you'd never guess Uncle Bryn and my father were brothers, they have almost nothing in common. Dad helps people getting divorced for a living and Bryn had an affair for thirteen years before marrying someone about thirty years his junior and having a child at sixty-five. Bryn is a magnificent sailor, whereas Dad once crashed a very small boat into a wall of rocks, even though the boat was in a completely placid lagoon, and the lagoon was in a resort, and even though his children were in it. Uncle Bryn fixes phone cabling for British Telecom, and Dad once tried to repair the roof with a pair of jeans. They really don't have anything in common, except their shared, and unique only unto them, way of dealing with the dead.

In the year 2000, Nanna Mildred died, unceremoniously on the couch, serenaded away by Alf and Pippa and an ashtray, her truest friends. Having not been given any adequate warning, my father was in Annandale at the time, and having been to all the previews of Nanna dying, alas, missed the feature.

My father boarded a plane, where he presumably shed some tears and thought about the woman that had brought him into the world until just after take off when the plane's entertainment system kicked in and his thoughts turned to Joey, Ross, Monica and the other *Friends* for the next twenty hours. When Dad arrived in Cardiff he got a taxi to Bryn's house. Bryn wasn't home. His wife told Dad that Bryn was at Nanna Mildred's cleaning up. Dad picked up the phone and called his mother's flat.

'Son! Is that really you?' A croaky, familiar high pitched voice answered. 'You've finally come to visit your poor old Mam?'

While Dad was mid confused aneurism, a hearty male laugh bellowed down the phone.

'Got you,' said Bryn. And the two brothers laughed and laughed because imitating their dead mother on the phone was fun, apparently. It started something of a pattern which was to characterise the time Dad spent in Cardiff cleaning up Nanna Mildred's flat and organising her funeral.

Bryn would call Dad from work, as Dad sat in the Council flat sifting through photos.

'Oh Bryn, is that you?' Dad would say from Nanna's phone. 'Now before you go to the discoteque you must help me wash all my knickers.'

Dad would call Bryn while Bryn was at the flat packing up Nanna's pots and pans.

'Paul did you know it was my birthday yesterday? I'm sure your card will come in the mail soon, when all the others come.'

And so on and so forth. I guess her funeral happened somewhere in there. Then the day came when Dad had to come home. He went back one last time to the council-brown Council flat, musty and beige, and sorted through all the yardage of lace and adult diapers and found a few trinkets and letters to cobble together to resemble some sort of inheritance.

When the Spanish first arrived in Mexico, they stumbled upon the Day of the Dead ceremony. Unlike the Spanish and many other peoples who considered death to be the end of life, the Mexicans thought death was only the beginning and instead of fearing death, they embraced it.

When Dad knocked on the door one last time, Uncle Bryn answered. Unlike the Mexicans, Uncle Bryn did not have a death mask or colourful hat. No. Uncle Bryn was wearing a housecoat and Nanna's wig. He had a fag dangling out his mouth and was hoovering the floor.

'Paul, you've come to visit me! Give your Mam a kiss,' said Uncle Bryn through the fag, leaning in for a smooch.

The Mexicans thought that life was a dream, and only in death did people become truly awake. Uncle Bryn and Dad had taken their own special and strange ritual to what may have been its natural conclusion. Drag. Maybe they were thinking about the wondrous unknowns of the after-life, that day, as they took turns dressing up as their dead mother. Or maybe they were just fucked.

A Zoë's Christmas in Annandale

By far the best and only significant element of Christmas day was the receiving of gifts purchased for you by a relative who is a relative stranger. A stranger who shared almost nothing with you. A stranger who wasn't sure what instrument you played, who wasn't sure if you were fat or lean, who wasn't sure if your ears were pierced, if you had enough beach towels, if you had enough sleeping bags, who'd settled on a sleeping bag and then couldn't quite remember if they'd already bought you a sleeping bag last year, that very sleeping bag, in that very same sale, not twelve months before.

A bag that's made for sleeping? A very sleeping bag! How I require both slumber and warmth, those are two things that I need every day! I shall put it with the others, for three is a collection. The pleasure of your gift accumulates slowly, would you buy it again? Surely not again? And once more with feeling! You are a patient gift-giving saint, but your efforts paid off, for I have a collection. Not quite as elegant, not quite as displayable as my stamp collection, but certainly warmer, certainly more zippery. Perhaps I will have them valued, perhaps I will clock them as assets on my next tax return, perhaps they will be in my dowry some day.

And what for my father? A man you know not well enough to phone or carry out a tête-a-tête one-on-one even for a few minutes? Even on Christmas day? Oh, why of course! Dark chocolate body paint, in a one-kilo tub! How did you know? How *did* you know?

And what for Mamma? A sixty-year-old woman with a serious job and a mortgage and a dishwasher? There's only one thing for such a woman. A belly-dancing skirt, made out of plastic coins painted gold. A skirt designed for maximum transparency, maximum exposure, both arse and fanny.

And what was Mamma to do, but try it on and shimmy through Christmas, and what was Father to do, but open the tub and offer a spoonful to a crying child.

That was Christmas, that *is* Christmas, the explosive pleasure of that singular feeling.

Christmas taught me why people light candles, why people like Joni Mitchell, why people wash their hands too much and forks go on the left, why we minute our silence and minute our steak, why we sleep on the same side, why we can be gluten free, why Papou gambles all our inheritance, why we wave Mexican and hello and goodbye and bury our dead and eat dessert after dinner: because tradition is sacred, tradition is always and its loss leaves the loser bereft and helpless, especially at Christmas.

It was a most sad day when just a week before Christmas, Mamma announced that the she had some news that might be painful. The extended family had decided to cancel the giving of Christmas presents. As the eldest and most traditional child at twenty-three, I was the least amused by this sacrilegious act, this unnecessary abuse. Didn't anyone understand? Once you take that away that tangible symbol of how little we know each other, we're no longer a family.

So just one week after this horrendous pronouncement, my family gathered in Mamma's house to act out this cicada-shell charade of Christmas, full to its edges with palpable emptiness.

And I start to wander off into my thoughts. I'm sitting alone at a bar and it's near closing and Lady Emptiness, dancing in a cage beckons me forth, shaking her beads – both worry and anal – come hither, come hither, let me show you my world. I look for a minute as she draws me in closer then I stare at her glistening body, dripping with glitter and beads and love. I see my reflection; I see the woe pulsating from the veins in my neck, from my watery shimmering eyes, from my rippling furrow-some brow. There has to be something else about Christmas, something else that makes me smile; that gives me joy. I think on it as I look at myself and then I remember just as I leave my daydream I've been dreaming around the Christmas table where everyone's eating. Children and adults drinking shandies and Pepsi and chattering into colourful plates, with their happy Christmas eyes and their jolly Christmas smiles that are gleaming with meat juice and just on cue, just as I remember, my Papou makes Christmas day okay. He sits upright like a peacock in his stretchy Christmas pants, his collared shirt and bib and he clears his throat.

'I'm so proud. All the women in my family have great tits,' he says. Everyone stops talking and my Yia Yia calls him an arsehole and one of the men gets up, slams his Christmas napkin on the table and says he's going for a walk. How could I forget, my fabulous Papou, drunken and sexist and loud and proud? He has the power. In twelve simple words spluttered out with flying droplets of beer and lamb gristle, he offends most injuriously to the point of protest. Papou winks at me, as if he somehow knows he's done me a good turn.

I take stock of myself with just enough time to realise that the man who's stormed out, who's been at every Christmas these last twenty-three years and given me so many inexplicable gifts, is such a stranger that I don't know his name. After all these years, I've never enquired how he's connected, who he's related to, why he's here. But now he's left to go and cool off because Papou offended his sensibilities and I'm feeling okay. How delightfully awkward not to know his name, the name of that man who deliciously left. Christmas is cooking even without those things we won't mention. It's like taking Herron Blue instead of Nurofen Plus. Not quite as numbingly wonderful, but not totally devoid of ibuprofen.

Next comes the big drunk sleep all the men and myself and any other women who are big drunk, sleep for a time on sofas and beds and floors. I notice when I rouse that people seem to be gone, where have they gone? All those women and children, un-drunk in Christmas garb? I quietly open a room in the house that is unofficially out of bounds, not on the tour of where Christmas happens. A room which contains only hats and a dart board, it's Father's special Hat room which Mamma doesn't deem fit for guests. I open the door, with the plan of stealing a fag from Father's sock draw.

And when I do a collective gasp and a dozen pairs of eyes greet me. Sitting frozen on the floor all in a circle, all the children and all their mothers, all of them except for the ones that live in this house, in my house, all of them sitting in a circle of gifts, gifts in big boxes and baskets and plastic. Surrounded by wrapping paper, batteries and sticky tape, bubble wrap, ribbon and stickers and bows. They look at me and don't know what to say. They had cancelled the giving of gifts for all, for all except everyone other than me, other than me and my family.

'We thought everyone was asleep,' says a young boy, the son of some lady. *Well done* think I to him, *well done for your explicit confirmation of what I already knew.*

And I consider for a moment how to capitalise, how to maximise this strange awkward feeling that's running through me like an electric dream.

'I thought we cancelled presents this year,' I say slowly and thoughtfully without any emotion, without letting them understand how I feel.

'Oh, it's just a few things.'

'A few little things.'

'It's nothing really.'

But you can't hide a bicycle with the back of your hand and you can't hide sheepishness on a dozen faces.

I decide to linger in the doorway in silence while they open their presents, and ruin their day. A Barbie car that transforms into a hotel. A portable DVD player. A pogo-stick. All big gifts, all *cool* gifts. Cool gifts exchanged between family members who *know* one another, who *like* one another. All gifts whose enjoyment must be silenced, because I am standing in the doorway ruining Christmas.

And all this time it wasn't the presents bringing me joy. I had focused so hard on the end game, that I'd no time to notice the beautiful journey. There are so many ways that Christmas is awkward, it is unpleasant and strange and bizarre. I still miss the presents, the ones I can keep, but they will fade and degrade with time, while awkwardness lives forever. I light a candle in my mind and sleep drunk on the couch, contented till second lunch.

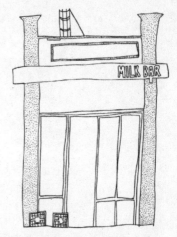

The Old Curiosity Shops

T o be truly at one with the human spirit is to watch it break. For a perfect expression of that singular sadness, I recommend witnessing a misguided small business open near your house and then see it close down very soon after.

You have seen this kind of business before, one that reeked with the stench of death. You might have noticed it for any number of reasons such as a spelling mistake in its name, disgusting decor, mean manager, inability to perform its primary commercial function – eg make coffee – stupid prices or too many rules.

Usually these ill-fated businesses sit alone. A little sinking ship upon a sea of relative profit. But not always.

That is something I learned the first time I moved out

of Annandale. Lovely little Annandale where every shop enjoys some measure of patronage, because, well it's just too darn sad otherwise.

I spent the better part of my twenties living in a terrace house right where two roads met. I lived there with some friends from uni and my boyfriend Mark.

I had fallen for Mark because he had done the manliest thing I had ever seen. On one of our first outings as a pair, Mark had taken me out on a little motor boat on a river. No sooner had we set off than I developed sea-panic and I grabbed onto an important part of the boat and snapped it off in my hand, causing the motor to break down. Then Mark jumped in the water, swam to an island, returned with a twig shaped like a fork. And fixed the motor. With a twig.

It transpired, I learned soon after, that once upon a time a genie had given Mark the ability to do one stupidly manly thing, once, and that was it. The entire rest of his life consisted of going into sudden states of paralysis when he saw a daddy-long-legs, spending twenty minutes dressing up like a psychotic yeti to scare away a wasp that had already flown out the window, and on the odd occasion when he'd attempt to fix something, saying things like, 'I'm just going to fix the door with the WD50,' which he did one time, before doing such a bad job that we became trapped *inside* our house and had to call a twenty-four-hour locksmith.

But nevertheless, we rubbed along. What Mark lacked in manly skills he made up for by designing cryptic crosswords, and being the best trivia player in the inner west. He also took a keen interest in my obsession with failing shops.

And so we moved in together with our friends. It wasn't so far from Annandale as the crow flies, our sharehouse, but when it came to community spirit, it couldn't have been more distant. In this strange, new place we didn't overfeed our homeless and we certainly didn't go into shops unless they sold good things.

There were a lot of terrible features about that house, like the mattress that somebody dragged in and left in the garden to function as both a squishy wall to piss up against and a grotesque slippery slide. But it also had a balcony that looked out onto a ruinous intersection, a little dogleg of crippled enterprise where every single shop had terrible wares, burned brightly and died quickly.

There was a bric-a-brac shop owned by a washed-up entertainer that sold items (which I assumed were) from her house because they were unpleasing to the eye, cost a fortune, and she agonised over parting with each of them. 'Fart Burgers' (diminutive), the hamburger-providore whose patties struck down even the strongest constitution into a night of explosive flatulence. Fruit On Vegetables, a grocer who didn't have a cash register and charged a flat fee of $4.60 for any purchase. There was a retro-furniture store, which was basically fine, but kamikazed by choosing only to open on Tuesdays and Wednesdays, nobody's favourite days to shop. There was a shop that only fixed clocks. A hair salon whose name, plastered across the whole shop-front, was composed in such a slanty-hand that it was indecipherable, rendering it impossible for anyone but a brave passer-by to make a booking. There was briefly a Far-East-inspired bazaar that sold incense, sequined cushions and lasagne, and a chiropractor who sold home-made peanut butter.

Discordance was a crucial signifier of doom. As a naïve school-bairn I had on occasion mocked the slogan 'This goes with that at Suzanne' but it turns out Ms Suzanne was a responsible investor. For a shop that sells items rarely seen together is either a bloody revolution, like the first café-bookstore, or it's going to be the reason somebody loses their house.

This was one of the things I observed peering over my balcony to skid row, in quiet, focused reflection, a horrible bird watcher who secretly wants all the birds to die.

Like any philosopher I would sometimes be moved to real feelings by my observations. As I would force myself to look out on the carnage below I would ask, who were these people's friends? Their family? Does anybody love them?

I would indulge in origin-story fantasies. I would picture the shop-keeper coming home and telling his wife about his big idea, I'd see him slowly bring her around, their first meeting with the bank, the signing of the lease, the arguments over Dulux swatches, their knuckles white as snow with opening day nerves. And then I would become depressed. I didn't ever need to finish the story – so familiar was I with the exact feeling of emptiness that was its inevitable end.

I also made mistakes.

I had once become over-curious about a café at the intersection that sold underwhelming landscape paintings and amber teething necklaces. One day I threw caution to the wind, entered the premises, ordered a takeaway latte and asked what was going on.

The gentleman mistook my line of questioning for hospitable neighbourly behaviour, rather than the spirit of hard empirical enquiry I was shooting for. He looked at me with a solemn gratitude.

'I painted these,' he said, pointing around the room to the childish watercolours. 'Do you like them?'

'Very much so.' I said, smiling. I learned his name was Roger, and I knew I'd made an egregious error.

'My wife makes these,' he said, holding up the baby-witchcraft. 'Amber teething necklaces are very important for babies. Do you have a baby?'

'No.'

'How old are you? You should think about a baby.'

I took my latte and left, and as I walked home I realised there was no way of getting to any of my regular errands without passing that café. And from the next morning for the ensuing several years I would have to pass that café every single day.

'Zoë!' Roger would call from across the street. 'Zoë! Coffee?'

'...Oh, yes please.'

I was more than capable of harsh judgement from my precious balcony, but not very good at it in real life and, as such, due to my initial mistake, I had a shitty coffee and a conversation about my ova every morning. And I made a note never again to fraternise with case studies.

Directly opposite my house were a convenience store and a Blockbuster. The convenience store thrived like a cockroach in a holocaust, even though the man behind the counter was a hopeless sleaze with a very unusual high-risk technique. He would project his perversions onto a plastic bag.

'You don't want a plastic bag? The plastic bag is very sad, and it wants to come home with you.'

But the convenience store sold the cigarettes and sugar, which the other depressed store-keepers needed, so it bucked the trend. Then there was the Blockbuster, which was fine for a long time, and then its industry died and it had to close down.

Enter Ristorante Lamborghini: a pizza parlour, which opened rather too quickly after the Blockbuster had closed. Too quickly, for instance, to remove the patented

Blockbuster-blue carpet which meant that anyone ordering a pizza was destined to be reminded of the porn they were about to consume with it. And within that fantasy was forever etched the man behind the mission, the man with the wax-twirled moustache, the ancient, withering Mr Lamborghini himself.

I was so curious about Ristorante Lamborghini, so curious it hurt, but I had been bitten and I vowed never to go inside. I did however order a Hawaiian pizza from Dominos in honour of its opening night that I observed from my balcony.

There was a rather large turnout. I watched as the premiere diners poured in, families with children, elderly couples and young ones too, in they came two by two then four by four, there was even a friendly looking dog tied out the front. Suddenly the place was full and waiters darted everywhere, somewhat unprepared for custom, all to the soundtrack of *Dean Martin's Greatest Hits* which blared on repeat. I was very taken aback by this apparent success, which defied all the behavioural patterns I had classified to date. But as I scrutinised the diners I created a hypothesis. That there were no neighbourhood faces, that the diners weren't happy hungry hippos at all. They were smiling dining plants who probably shared a bloodline with Mr Lamborghini.

My speculation was validated by what happened over the rest of the week. Each night the number of diners halved and then quartered until what was left was one blessed family who came night after night after night until they eventually stopped, probably because they killed one of their children through carb-loading.

And then there was nothing. Nothing except *Dean Martin's Greatest Hits* which would start at five o'clock every day until close.

Nobody came in. Nobody came out.

Eventually all the staff were let go and Mr Lambourghini dangled over the front window, a cigarette drooping out of his mouth as he whiled away his days in deep sighs.

It was too much for me. I decided to shut up the lab and migrate inside until this winter of discontent had blown over.

One day Mark came home with a pizza in a plain, white box.

'Is that...?'

'Yes,' he said, 'I had to do it once.'

Mark was far more adventurous in the food department than I. He would sometimes eat chicken from a can and once had a dinner of a packet of Toobs, a piece of fudge and a tall glass of vodka. But somehow this was a new low.

He opened the box. Inside was a hideous misappropriation of a pizza. The thing was to a pizza what Cecilia's Borja fresco is to an actual fresco, with peperoni where talent should have been.

We looked at each other.

'I thought it was strange, I don't think the man used the oven.'

'What do you mean?'

'Well, I couldn't really see properly, but I'm pretty sure the man heated this up in a microwave.'

I looked at the sloppy monstrosity and concluded that Mark was probably right. Mr Lamborghini was so depressed he'd lost his will to turn on the oven.

Mark still ate it, of course.

Mr Lambourghini continued to open the shop at five o'clock every day and wait for nothing to happen.

After some months, there was a development. Mr Lamborghini would still open his shop, he would still play Dean Martin, but he repositioned himself on our side of the street and he would sit on the stoop outside our house smoking his perpetual cigarette and watching his dreams die.

One day Mark and I came home and found Mr Lamborghini motionless in his car, slumped over the steering wheel, his glistening bald head resting on the dashboard. His shop was open, the music playing. Was he dead? We had no idea.

We shouldn't do nothing, I remember thinking. So I rapped hard on the window with my bottle of Diet Coke. Mr Lamborghini woke with a start.

He wound down his window.

'Do you want pizza?'

'No thanks, we just wanted to see if you were okay.'

'Oh,' he said. 'Thank you.'

He got out of the car and briefly examined his tomato-paste stained shirt. He wiped his bristling dark eyebrows with the back of his hand and he went back into his shop and decided to close it down.

I only spoke to Mr Lamborghini one more time after that. I had crossed the street and Mr Lamborghini was clearly very distressed as he yelled at a young man in a suit who wanted to buy the shop.

'You can't take them, the pictures are mine!' Mr Lamborghini was standing in front of a poster of a Lamborghini, blocking the man.

'I don't want the stupid poster. I want to take a picture.' He said motioning a camera with his hands.

'It's alright,' I said to Mr Lamborghini, 'he wants a photo of the shop.'

'Ok.' He said, embarrassed and he wandered out the back.

'He really made a mess of this place,' the man said.

'Yeah,' I said. 'What are you going to do with it?'

'I sell climbing plants and antiques,' he said and then he motioned with his hand across the shop window. 'It's called Vinetique.'

'Good luck with that,' I said.

Petrol

Quite a big chunk of my life has been spent sitting in the passenger seat of our various family cars. We had a lot of cars, but not all at the same time like a fancy family with a fleet. Rather we had a succession of shit cars that would require replacing frequently. We'd love each car dearly but in all the wrong ways then we'd panic and kill it.

The car we had for the longest was Crap Car. Crap Car lived under the shade of our jacaranda tree which covered her in a blanket of regal oily purple and ultimately stripped her paint. We lined her boot with rotting beach towels and clothes that weren't good enough for the charity bin, then we'd stuff the raggedy boot full of possums and release them somewhere that wasn't our house.

Crap Car's seats bore the smell and stains of a hundred spilled lattes and her walls wore the scars of a thousand arguments about directions and why we weren't stopping at McDonald's, about air conditioning, world capitals, sleepovers, over who had stolen whose bra and who just bitch-slapped who first in the back seat.

Very much against her will, we would force a cassette into her every day. A cassette which played 'That's Amore' on repeat, and we'd sing with such offence and repetition that she would overheat her own cassette deck and try to melt it. But we'd pull it out, blow on it, wind the curly black tape back in and jam it back in her again, each time a little harder.

Crap Car used to stop suddenly on the freeway and start billowing out ghastly black smoke. I always assumed she waited until she was in broad daylight in a large crowd of her peers where she felt safe to alert everyone to the fact that she was being tortured at home. When the NRMA men would come to take her away we'd make up excuses for her pitiful state, we'd sign the forms, we'd get her back and we'd do her over again.

Crap Car was so depressed that her ceiling began to collapse in on us, like the flopping dorsal fin of a tortured Seaworld orca. On her final trip to the fixer, when she was no longer fit for purpose, she was given to the mechanic's sixteen-year-old son to do with what he pleased. I can only assume this meant a better life.

We promised ourselves we'd be nicer to the next car. And we were. Opi was the closest thing to having pedigree of any member of our family. She was tiny and golden and had been bought from the Carringtons, a nice old couple who only drove her to the Booth Street shops once a week, and who didn't know a swindler when my Dad came to offer them a significantly less-than-market-value price for her. We loved Opi. Only coffees with lids could hitch a ride in that trusty mare. And we would gently put inside her a cassette with five different songs on it; two Travelling Wilburys tracks, one Aqua's 'Barbie Girl', an excerpt from the *Chicago* soundtrack and, of course, 'That's Amore'. A month into this arrangement, Opi seemed happy, contented and clean. Then one day when she was quietly parked out the front of our house, a 4WD drove straight into her side at some speed and wrote her off completely. We were devastated. And we adopted what I understand to be a popular, yet unhealthy way to deal with grief: we replaced her with something that looked quite similar, but that we would never love in the same way. Her name was Ark.

Recently I was sitting in the front passenger seat of Ark. Mamma was driving, because, frankly, I don't know how to. It seems very hard. Mamma is very sympathetic to my lack of driving ability and is always quick to accept a lift-request, particularly if the journey involves coffee, stopping at a wool shop, dress shop, jewellery shop or shoe shop, or sneaking into an auction to see if anything interesting goes down. She sometimes even drives me to her most hated place in the world: Kmart. Car trips with Mamma are where we do most of our relationship, especially if it's hard to find a park that doesn't require reversing which can sometimes lengthen our adventures by some twenty minutes. Mamma has always been very supportive of everything I do, like maxing out my credit card, choosing a nonsense career and never learning how to drive.

One muggy summer afternoon, at the tender age of thirty, I am driving around with Mamma who is taking me for a spin around Annandale. Having gone back and forth several times from the nest, I am at this point enjoying a stint of living out of home like an Adult. But if anything, this makes me more needy of Mother's constant care. In the backseat of the car is a new set of forks, because Mamma noticed I only had two at home, which was not enough for an Adult. The forks are sitting atop my freshly laundered-by-Mamma bed sheets and next to them is a little basket with fresh pasta and strawberries she's brought me from the market to stave off the scurvy I may be on the brink of developing from only consuming cheese sandwiches and wine for the past fortnight.

When we pull into the petrol station, I ask Mamma to wind up the windows to stymie the thick, summer sticky petrol smell, even though it would inevitably seep through into Ark's confines anyway. I am sitting in the car waiting for Mamma to come back when I hear the slightly dulled, but distinct sound of a woman screaming. I do the responsible thing and ignore it. I ignore it until the screams crystalise into a sound I recognise.

'ZOOOOOOOOOOOOOOOOOËËËËËËËËËËË ËËËË!!!!!!!!!!!!!'

I turn around in my seat and can make out the shape of my mother through the window. She is dancing. Mamma is screaming my name and she is dancing.

I open the door and step out of the car. I look around. I look around at all of the men and women who are standing flush against their cars, bidding their children stay inside. Their faces, wretched with terror.

Mamma holds the petrol gun high in the air as she dances and screams my name over and over.

She is dripping wet, and doing a mangled two-step in her petrol-squelching loafers and screaming as her red and orange floral Mexican night-dress turns an oily shade of see-through, and her whispy black bob mats down on her face.

It transpired that Mamma, having filled up a car once a week for the past forty years, had somehow, I still don't know how, completely forgotten the basic principles of that task. That, and some key mechanism in the pump (which I can only assume exists), to stop petrol spewing out when it's not in use had busted. Whatever combination of factors, Mamma had managed to douse herself from head to toe in petrol, giving her the appearance of a very dangerous person who urgently needs to be tasered.

213

But with no policeman in sight and a little scene of frightened Annandaleans doing nothing at all, it seemed that this task was to fall to me.

'Give. Me. The Gun.' I said, loudly, but with a certain calm assertion. And I approached the maniac, as the other patrons drew back.

'I DON'T KNOW WHAT HAPPENED!'

'Just give me the gun, woman. Now.'

I walked at her slowly, arms outstretched. Then I grabbed the gun from her flailing arm and restored it to Ark's petrol hole.

The petrol hole! I was using the petrol hole! I had never filled up a car before, and a warm sense of power came over me.

'Get in the car,' I said to her.

'I can't get in the car! I'm covered in petrol. I'M COVERED IN PETROL,' screamed the beast, as she lunged at a man who had stopped cleaning his car to watch the terrifying spectacle. She grabbed the warm bucket of soapy grime water the man had been using to clean his hub caps and held it to herself.

'Don't do it!' I shouted. 'You'll make things worse!'

'THEY CAN'T GET ANY WORSE!' screamed Mamma as she tipped the disgusting bucket over her head.

And then she stood there breathless, and see-through, soapy and petrolly in her Mexican night-dress.

'Get in the fucking car, right now,' I said, still in mild

shock at my own apparent capacity to stick the petrol gun in the petrol hole.

'You need money to pay!'

'Just get in the car. We'll talk about this later.'

I grabbed Mamma's wallet and went into the petrol station. I picked up a Diet Coke and a family-sized chocolate bar and took them to the counter.

'I need to pay for the petrol,' I said, trying to sound casual.

'What number?' asked the Man.

'I don't know what you mean, but it's for the car with the screaming, wet woman. '

'Number three,' said the Man. 'If you buy four Diet Cokes the fifth one is free,' he continued, seemingly unphased by Mamma's attempted self-immolation incident.

I paid and left. I climbed back into the passenger's seat. My role as Fill-In Boss of the Car was over. Mamma squelched her petrol sodden loafer on the accelerator and we drove towards home.

It was just after three and the streets were flapping with children out of school. We turned into our street, and a man in his car with three kids started racing towards us, ramping himself up for the inevitable who-goes-backsies in the narrow really-shouldn't-be two way street. He was clearly in for a fight this man, as he pressed ever forward, trying to push us backwards onto the main road. He tooted at Mamma and shook his head. She calmly wound down the window and said, 'Hello. I'm covered in petrol. I suggest you fuck off backwards.'

Which he did.

We got in the house.

Mamma reached into her purse. I wasn't sure what she was doing, clearly the only thing she needed to do was have a shower, but much to my horror she pulled out her little gold cigarette case. She opened it up, tapped a cigarette on the metal, put it in her mouth and then held up a lighter.

'WHAT THE FUCK ARE YOU DOING?' I blared.

'Just kidding,' she said, 'I'm not crazy.'

Yía Yía on Papou

If my name is Koula and your name is Mick and we shall be met and we shall be married under the auspices of the father in the Greek Orthodox Parish and Community of Saints Raphael, Nicholas and Irene, then you shall remember this, you shall remember this forever, and if you shall remember this, then you may begin to understand my eternal contempt.

If my name is Koula and your name is Mick and we shall be met and we shall be married and we shall cohabitate in a house-familius in Suburbingford with our two children and our patio and our various Shih tzus named Dadie and Sadie and similar, and our Carlton Ware, our plastic-covered couches, our china horses, cups of tea, brass statuette of the Harbour Bridge, our security blinds and tobacco, our flannelettes and mouthwash.

If one day in this situation unto which we have found ourselves you shall ask unto me: Koula, *pou ine tou alago thacktilithi mou* favourite? I will say: How the fuck should I know Mick. If it's not on your *butso-glifti* finger, then *pous thialo* would I know where your stupid favourite ring with the horseshoe is?

If you shall suggest that blame for this ring misplacement lies outside the gelatinous boundaries of yourself, perhaps with me or our children or our Shih tzus and you shall make us search the house.

If one day, two weeks after you have lost the ring, and we have searched the house, you shall cry out unto me from your seat on the toilet, whilst peering southward, with a repulsive strain over your gut, down to your knee-ward underpants: Koula! *Do echo vriso. Ine sta Y-Front vrakya mou!*

If you shall find, sitting there in your underpants your favourite horseshoe ring, understand that I shall know you have not changed your underpants for two weeks. Understand that the fact that you did not notice a ring with a jagged horseshoe setting burring into your buttocks for two weeks suggests a disturbing deficit in observation and a medically significant lack of somatic response in your fat arse. You should see several kinds of doctors.

Furthermore, understand Mick, understand that I have never lost anything. Understand that I have no sympathy for you. Understand this and you shall begin to understand the emergence of my eternal contempt.

If my name is Koula and your name is Mick and we have been met and we have been married and you have no feeling in your arse and one day you tell me you are taking our seven-year-old son to the Maritime Museum.

If, instead of taking him to the museum, you leave him in the car for four hours while you drink at the RSL with other arseholes like you, who you are friends with because you all share ninety per cent of your genes with elephant seals.

If you do this Mick, our son will remember forever, and I will never forget. And when you are old and vague and I am old, I shall carry my blackened memories of you forever in my mouth ulcers.

If my name is Koula and your name is Mick and we have been married and you have no feeling in your arse and you have previously left our son in a car for four hours and you are sixty-eight and you are not dead and I have not forgotten and we are flatting together for apathy and convenience.

If one day in this situation unto which we have found ourselves, you shall suppose to comment on my cooking

If one day you shall squint and wheeze as the pencil shavings and hairy sodden bath-plugs comprising your brain attempt to inhale, interpret and re-release information back into the ether. If your brain shall miraculously evade electrocution through unprecedented usage, and you manage to sneeze out of your teeth bucket the premature stillborn of a would be verbalised thought. Should this premi-thought call into the arena of question an aspect of my cooking. Understand this. Understand that everyday for fifty years, I have, in spite of the emergence and subsequent exponential growth of my eternal contempt cooked you three perfect meals everyday. Understand that perfection is my only weakness. Understand that my kitchen has a fucking chef's hat. And understand that in order to ensure that nothing of this sort recurs I shall beat you repeatedly over the head with a Christmas placemat.

If my name is Koula and your name is Mick and we have been met and we have been married and you have no feeling in your arse and you once left our seven-year-old son in the car and I have beaten almost every last drop of your ambition to engage with the world out of your head with a Christmas placemat and you are seventy-five and you are not dead and I have not forgotten.

If one morning before dawn, in this situation unto which we have found ourselves, I encounter you in our driveway, with a garbage bag full of tissues and ornaments, wearing nothing but a pair of white stubbies, waiting for your eight-year-old grandson to drive you to your lacrosse game. Understand that you seem to have gone completely mad. Understand that the only upsetting part of this situation for me is that I briefly had to look at you without a shirt on.

If my name is Koula and your name is Mick and we have been met and we have been married and you have no feeling in your arse and one day you left our son in the car and I have beaten your churlishness with a Christmas placemat and you have gone mad and you have disappointingly recovered quickly and we have moved to *stou thiavolou ti manna* retirement villa and one day you sit at your window sill, staring at the happenstance in your visual field, and you shall say: 'Koula, you have to come and see this. There is a little white dog, just sitting there on the grass. It's so still. I wonder if it's lonely. It's so beautiful. *Parakalo* Koula.'

And I will refuse.

'*Parakalo*.'

'No.'

'*Parakalo*, just one little look.'

'No.'

'Koula…'

'Fine. Mick,' I will say as I disgust myself by eventually humouring you.

'Mick that is a FUCKING MAILBOX.'

Understand that if you mention how low your cholesterol is in spite of eighty years of treating your body like a hospital-grade bag of infected rubbish, understand that if Lady Life renews her lease on you, and you develop a penchant for 'walks', understand that in bitterness, in unbridled bitterness, I shall have a segment of my lower bowel removed.

223

If my name is Koula and your name is Mick and one day having served you lunch I shall ask for a sip of your beer.

If I shall ask for but one sip of your beer and you shall look me in the eyes, you shall look me in the eyes with sixty-five years of hatred, you shall look me in the eyes and I shall meet your eyes, and without taking your eyes off me you shall pick up the beer in your pig hand and take it to your pink and crusty, discarded by the butcher and left in the sun poisoned ham lips. And you shall swig from it.

If you shall swig from it and then exhale beer, particles of lunch, and air all at once. If then, after this brothel performance you shall offer unto me your beer, I will put a curse on you.

If after I put a curse on you, you shall summon, from within your gingivitis cavernous death-pot mouth, a phlegmatic viscous. If you shall spit this phlegmatic viscous and chart it on a course toward my face. If you shall do this Mick, then understand you shall have regrets.

If my name is Koula and your name is Mick and one day you spit in my face. Understand that with all my will I will reach behind me for a knife. Understand that if all I can place my hands upon without looking, without unlocking our hating eyes, understand that if I cannot reach a knife, if all I can reach is a colander, understand that I shall use the colander like a sort of knife hat. And I shall drive it onto your head.

And there you shall be, drunk and vague with nothing but your colander-hat and what remains of your beer and the dishrag of your soul.

Mick, if you understand these things, if you understand them, then you shall begin to understand me and my eternal contempt.

Zoë was born in Annandale in 1984, where she was essentially a normal person until she went to a Performing Arts High School where she received an A for Wanker, a B+ for Smoking and a Dolphin for Maths.

For more than twenty years, Zoë's parents held the record for the biggest unpaid fine at the Annandale Video Shop. Due to legal reasons and the fact that the sheer number of numbers required to write the fine's dollar figure here would destroy the pagination of this book, we will not disclose the actual fine. We only ask that you imagine the biggest number you can think of then add to that all of the stars in the sky and all of the times anyone has ever said 'I love you' then double it. The only challenge to the title Worst Fine™, came when her sister, Little Georgia was issued her own video renting card. She managed to come within $██████████████████ (redacted, Ed.) of her parents' record, but was taken out of contention when her highly competitive parents went behind Little Georgia's back and paid it off, having no interest in being out-fined by an infant.

Until very recently, when she had reason to examine her birth certificate, Zoë thought there was an umlaut above the ë in her name, which there apparently is not. She has no idea what possessed her parents to lie to her on this matter for thirty years, allowing her to spell her name with this pretentious fiction, but Zoë deeply fears change so the umlaut stays.

Zoë is also a writer and presenter on *The Checkout* and *The Chaser's Media Circus* (ABC1), creator of the hit sellout live event-cum-highly obscure TV show *Story Club* (ABC2) and has had her work published in many Australian literary journals including *Best Australian Stories*.

Some of the stories in this collection have appeared in *The Best Australian Stories* (2012), *Going Down Swinging #32*, *The Penguin Plays Rough Book of Short Stories*, *Seizure*, *Between Us: Women of Letters* (2014).

Zoë would also like to give a big smooch of gratitude to everybody who makes Story Club possible.

This project has been assisted by the Commonwealth Government through the Australia Council, its arts funding and advisory body.